Cover Letters That Will
Get You the Job You Want

ABOUT THE AUTHOR

Stanley Wynett is uniquely qualified for the role of advice-giver to jobhunters: He has been a job applicant, an employer, and a writer for mass readership. As president of Stan Wynett Resumes, the largest resume writing and job counseling firm in New York City, Wynett has written resumes and cover letters for mail carriers to presidents—and for many of the top executives in Manhattan, on Wall Street, and in banking, broadcasting, and retailing.

From his years of experience, Wynett knows that most job applicants do not know *how* to write an effective resume and cover letter because they simply do not know what an employer looks for in screening job applicants. So they do the easiest thing and copy someone else's. The single most common mistake, and one that is made remarkably often, is listing duties rather than *accomplishments*. "An employer will read six pages of accomplishments," Wynett says, "but no more than a page of duties, if that."

In addition to his counseling and writing through Stan Wynett Resumes, Wynett is also the author of *Cues, Schmooze & Taboos About Job Interviews* and numerous articles for the *National Business Employment Weekly*.

Drawing by C. Barsotti; © 1989
The New Yorker Magazine, Inc.

" 'I yam what I yam an' that's all I yam!' What
the hell kind of cover letter is that?"

Cover Letters That Will Get You the Job You Want

STANLEY WYNETT

BETTER WAY BOOKS

CINCINNATI, OHIO

Other fine Betterway Books are available from your local bookstore or direct from the publisher.

Cartoon drawing on page ii by C. Barsotti; © 1989. The New Yorker Magazine, Inc.

02 01   9 8 7 6

Library of Congress Cataloging-in-Publication Data

Wynett, Stanley.
    Cover letters that will get you the job you want / Stanley Wynett.—1st ed.
      p.   cm.
    Includes index.
    ISBN 1-55870-275-X (pbk.)
    1. Applications for positions. 2. Cover letters. 3. Job hunting. I. Title.
HF5383.W96   1993
808'.066651—dc20   92-45218
                                           CIP

Edited by Jack Heffron
Designed by Sandy Conopeotis

Dedication

I dedicate this book to the cover letter itself. This beautiful instrument permits you, the jobhunter, to control totally any prospective employer's first impression of you.

Everything that shows how good you are is put in. Anything that could possibly hurt you is left out. What is the result to be? What else can it be? The cover letter is made to order for all the purposes of jobhunters.

There is almost nothing you can't do with a cover letter, yet most people choose to do nothing.

The 100 cover letters included in this book landed hundreds of interviews. Each bumped up against 40-600 other applicants in the same mail, competing for the same position. Moreover, all of the letters were written and used between 1990-92, a period of deep joblessness and recession in the United States, which merely shows that well-written cover letters work to bring interviews in good times and bad.

The 100 letters are the combined writing products of the customers of my resume writing service and me. Customers brought their cover letters to me for evaluation, and decided to rewrite. The thoughts and statements in these letters are largely those of the authors. If the letters sound like real-life situations, it's because they are real. My participation consisted of writing the actual drafts, weaving together the principles outlined in this book and the letter writer's own words.

These letters were successful because they promised employers some benefit the employers really wanted, and thus they *made* time to read them.

Perhaps you've already discovered that some executives are better guarded than kings and ministers. Yet you can use your cover letter to travel on paper past their secretaries who ask phone callers in a chilling, inquiring voice, "What is this call in reference to?" and then tell you your quarry is not in, is engaged, is in a meeting, is this or is that, but is not available to you.

The techniques and devices I give you in this book, properly applied to only mildly interesting job achievements, can appeal to employers and attract them to read your cover letter almost against their will. The appeals are based on known and proven principles of just what stimuli it takes to arrest an employer's attention. You'll be able to tap into the hopes and fears—and greed—of employers to impel them to grant the interviews you desire.

The intangibles of communication on paper—the *vibes* it produces—are much more vital to your success than the mere words themselves. E. B. White, coauthor of *The Elements of Style*, said, "Merely to learn that it's not all *what* you say, but *how* you say it is to take a long stride."

This may come as a surprise to you, but the words and phrases you choose show employers your temperament and aspirations, even your outlook on life. You are encouraged in how-to-get-a-job books to take your personality *out* of your writing in your resume, but your cover letter is to be used exclusively for putting it back in. Psychologists, too, have long analyzed language as a key to personality. Every college admissions office asks applying students to submit a page or two of their writing on some assigned topic.

Don't get me wrong. Solid achievements in the workplace are the mainspring of everything. But every job opening brings in hundreds of responses. Unless your cover letter stands out, employers may be totally unaware of you. You will see how clearly and memorably you can express yourself on paper to a prospective employer—to anyone.

It's safe for you to standardize a large part of your letter

In *How to Write A Good Advertisement*, Victor Schwab tells an anecdote about Alexander Dumas, who wrote *The Three Musketeers*. Dumas is said to have copied in longhand—100 times—everything he wrote. No matter how well he liked the 50th draft, every single thing he wrote was copied 100 times to be sure he still liked it. I will spare you that.

It is extremely safe for you to standardize a large part of your cover letter. Change the opening when that seems desirable. But there is no reason why the main part of your story has to be rewritten over and over, once you have found the most effective way to present it. You can merge your own ideas with the prewritten examples and originate letters that are truly yours and tell your unique story.

You won't ever again have to face a blank page, and wonder how you can write a thoughtful response to an ad you saw in today's newspaper. You'll find everything you need in this book to make lasting impressions with your letters. You have practical, tested material right at your fingertips. You will eliminate time-consuming searches for lead-ins, themes and closes. You'll be surprised at how easily it will all come to you. You'll know just what you are going to say.

I intend to show you small, simple steps that will change almost any self-limiting writing patterns virtually overnight. Big changes will appear in the way you write.

If you abide by the hints, tips and suggestions in this book, you will find yourself pulling employers toward you as a magnet attracts iron filings. Onward!

CHAPTER 1
The Cover Letter's Unique Advantages

Only 20% of jobs are advertised. "Where are the other 80%?" you may well ask.

The other 80% consist of openings in the making. They may be brand new jobs, the result of expanded business, which have been in the planning stages but not yet publicized. Or, they may be existing positions that have reached the we-must-do-something-about-replacing-so-and-so stage. Or maybe someone is about to be promoted. Or someone is leaving to take another job.

Your cover letter helps you penetrate the hidden job market

Not infrequently, even the human resources department has not yet been advised that a manager is considering adding to the staff or replacing someone. Your uninvited cover letter seeking a position may be welcomed with cheers by the manager because it offers a solution to the staffing problem without having to compose and place an expensive ad, without having to contact employment agencies or recruiters, with hardly any exertion at all on the part of the manager. Think it over.

Tom Jackson and Davidyne Mayleas say in their brilliant book, *The Hidden Job Market* (Quadrangle/ *New York Times* Books, 1976):

> For years most people have felt that the jobs that exist for them are those which are shown in today's classified section, or in the employment agency listings. It is now recognized that on any given day, only 10 to 15

percent of the available job openings are listed in the newspaper or with agencies. There is another, vastly larger reservoir of jobs and opportunities available. These are the thousands of positions which are in the process of being created.

The Only Job Hunting Book You'll Ever Need, by Kathryn and Ross Petras (Poseidon Press, 1989), quotes an employer: "We always have jobs for the right people, even if officially we're not hiring."

These hidden but soon-to-be-available jobs are obtainable by some assertive person like yourself who is right for the job and mails a letter saying so to the person doing the hiring.

You announce your availability for the job, and offer the achievements that make you worthy of it. If you fit the qualifications the employer has in mind, you will be asked in for an interview. Or your letter and resume may be kept on file for review later. In penetrating the hidden job market, a resume accompanied by a sparkling cover letter is five times as effective as a resume mailed alone.

Executive recruiters prefer cover letters

It may help you to understand the importance attached to a cover letter when writing to executive recruiters if I quote here a few sentences from John Sibbald's *The Career Makers—America's Top 100 Executive Recruiters* (Harper & Row, 1990). He confirms how dogged job applicants must be to get the attention of the top executive recruiters:

> Tough as the odds are of using a resume to start building the all-important relationship with the right recruiters, there are some ways to dramatically improve your chances. It comes down to basic marketing; you've got to have a handle. The handle we're talking about can best be presented in the cover letter that accompanies your resume. But most important is what the cover letter says and to whom. Virtually all resumes that reach our top recruiters are accompanied by cover letters. Yet not one cover letter in fifty contains an effective handle. *Finding the handle that makes your resume stand out to the right executive recruiters is the single most important objective for smart jobseekers today.* (Italics in original.)

Sibbald defines *handle* as "a special attraction that positions you and causes you to be selected from all the other products on the shelf." You are wise enough to see there is something in his advice.

Few retained recruiters will accept phone calls from executives they don't know. Instead most prefer candidates send a cover letter and resume.

Cover letters help overcome a variety of job-hunting problems

No previous work experience. If you are a recent graduate, chances are you may have little paid work experience in the career of your choice. For you, a resume is more of a hindrance than a help, because it spotlights what a recent graduate often *does not* have—any sort of paid work experience related to the job sought.

A cover letter has this advantage: It highlights only those things that make you seem a fit candidate for the job, and everything else that could distract the reader and hurt your interview chances is left out.

Changing careers. Of the over 500 cover letters my firm helped jobhunters prepare last year, the third largest category we worked on was *changing careers*. Employers are apprehensive about jobhunters who are switching into their field after spending time in another. A reassuring cover letter relating the skills you possess to the skills the employer requires helps smooth your way. (See Chapter 9.)

Moving to a new city or country. Another complication a jobhunter has to explain away is moving to a new location. Why are you leaving, weren't you successful? Are you hiding anything? Why didn't anyone there want to hire you? How long would you stay with us? (See Chapter 9.)

Masking age. A cover letter is far better suited than a resume for masking age. No custom requires that dates be furnished or chronological order be observed in a cover letter, whereas both are strictly required in a resume.

Not having to give dates permits you to go back into your career as much as 20 or 30 years for accomplishments, while giving them the appearance of being current. This is a true advantage the cover letter offers to anyone who is no longer young.

Cover letters permit you to personalize ad responses

Answering employers' ads with a resume accompanied by a cover letter is a highly productive way of gaining interviews. A well-composed cover letter can vault you ahead of the hundreds who apply for the advertised position, because most jobhunters respond to ads automatically and blindly. Let me prove this.

Your cover letter allows you to give the employer precisely what the employer's ad is looking for. This is a flexibility feature of the cover letter the preprinted resume cannot duplicate, unless it is rewritten continually. (Ninety-eight percent of jobhunters use a single resume to apply for any and all job openings that come to their attention.)

For example, you see an ad for a job you know

you are right for. But the ad's five requirements are covered in different places on your resume, and not underlined or italicized to stand out. Not to worry.

Your cover letter permits you to address the ad's five specific requirements, and match them to your experience, point by point. Each of those requirements you see in the ad are skills, experience or personality traits the employer values most. You now have targets to zero in on. The employer decides you are a contender for the position and turns to read your resume.

Incidentally, maybe a requirement of the ad that you do not possess makes you feel there is no use in your answering. Respond anyway—a desirable outcome is *possible*. Employers rarely find their dream candidate—one with strong abilities in *each* of their requirements. Often employers may value a single virtue more than the others combined, and that may be the area in which you excel.

Just remember, when you fall short of meeting all the requirements set forth in an ad, your response is a *reach* . . . not a perfect fit. So don't be hard on yourself or rewrite your basic letter if you do not score as many interviews with reach situations as you do responding to jobs you are right for (you fulfill *all* of an ad's requirements). The finest letter written may not cause the interview gates to swing open if you lack one or two of the job requirements stated in an ad that are accompanied by the words *must have* or *required*.

Summary

Both the cover letter and the resume are essentials of the job hunt, but the cover letter performs all sorts of tasks the resume cannot. I say with confidence a well-written cover letter can lift you from the densest obscurity to beat out your competitors and command the attention of employers of your choice.

CHAPTER 2

Mechanical Requirements and Proper Punctuation

In this chapter are the mechanical guidelines to make your letter look pretty on paper and inviting to read. Along with those, there are some simple rules of punctuation to be learned that tell your reader you know how to use the English language correctly. Many of these rules you know already. The rest are explained by example and easily implemented.

Mechanical requirements

Stationery. White paper, 25 lb. bond, 8½″×11″, is the overwhelming preference. Ivory is another acceptable color choice. Shades of gray (or any other color) are discouraged because the lack of contrast makes them harder to read. Use black ink. Colored inks (e.g., blue, brown) are distracting.

Ninety-eight percent of cover letters and resumes are printed in black ink on white paper, so it is only natural for you to feel that a change of color will show your originality and a wish to depart from the old way of doing things. Employers look for innovation and novelty in your *writing* and your *ideas*; they are not impressed by superficial, cosmetic changes in writing paper or color of ink. Stick with white, and you can't go wrong.

Printed letterhead. You will notice all the letters used as examples in this book have printed letterheads—a modest expense and a great convenience. Your phone number is placed last on your letterhead, so it is quickly seen. Almost all interviews are arranged by phone.

The words *street*, *avenue*, and so forth should be spelled out in your letterhead, e.g., 125 Front Street, not St.

It is acceptable, however, for you to abbreviate these words in the inside address (see section on Inside Address).

Margins. Leave at least 1½ inches on all four sides. It makes the body of the text *seem* less. If your message is brief, consider using two inches. The margin at the bottom of the page should never be less than two inches.

Date. Space down three spaces from the line on which your phone number appears. Type the date on the right half of the page. I prefer the right-hand side instead of flush with the left margin simply to break up the layout. The name of the month is spelled out, e.g., July 15, 1993. This is the preferred manner of writing dates in formal correspondence in the United States.

If you like the military (as well as European) style of writing dates, the order is day, month, year, e.g., 15 July 1993; it is an acceptable second choice. Less acceptable is writing the date with all numerals, e.g., 4/15/93. This format is better suited to internal memos, invoices, etc., where informality and time-saving are more in order.

Spacing. All text is single spaced. Double space between paragraphs. Double space when introducing a listing. The first line of each new paragraph is indented five spaces.

In writing brief letters, such as a thank-you note, where there are no more than a dozen lines, you may care to double space all the text in the body of your letter, with two-inch borders right and left.

Inside address. The inside address is a formality required in business correspondence that follows a standard format:

Mr. William A. McFarland, Jr. (name)

National Sales Manager (title)

Chemical Coatings Division (subsidiary, division, department, etc.)

Sun Chemical Co., Inc. (organization name / okay to abbreviate Co. and Corp. / comma precedes Inc.)

1200 Beechwood Blvd. (okay to abbreviate street, avenue, etc.)

Redlands, CA 01875 (city, state, zip code — no comma is needed between state and zip)

Salutation. "Dear . . ." has been used millions of times, but is still customary, accepted and expected as the salutation of choice for cover letters. The salutation is always punctuated with a colon at the end. There are two types of titles you may choose from in business correspondence. One is courtesy (Mr., Mrs., Ms.); the second is professional (Dr., Professor, Judge, Senator, Principal, etc.). If the person to whom you are writing has earned a professional title, by all means use it:

Dear Ms. Thompson: / Dear Mr. Drexler: / Dear Mrs. Kane:

Dear Dr. Katz: / Dear Professor Schuette: / Dear Captain Morrison:

Suppose you want a generic salutation applying to all executives in a job category, so you will be spared the bother of addressing each employer individually? Or, suppose you are responding to a box number where the employer's name is not revealed? Simply direct your salutation to the title of the person likely to head the department you will be working for:

Dear sales manager: / Dear customer relations director:

Or:

To the chief financial officer: / To the MIS director:

The salutation is typed two spaces below the last line of the inside address. Allow two more spaces between the salutation and the beginning of your first paragraph. Only the first word of the salutation is capitalized.

Complimentary close. I recommend using the single word *Sincerely*. The complimentary close is typed two spaces below the last line of your letter, and is always followed by a comma.

Signature. Write your name carefully and clearly so it can be read instantly. If the reader has to decipher a scrawled name written speedily and without concern for legibility, it smacks of ego, pomposity, vanity.

The next time you get a sales letter of any kind in the mail, glance at the signature. If you do not find it highly legible in every case, I will be very much surprised. When your letter asks something of the recipient, you want to provide the reader with no cause whatever for irritation.

Punctuation

Here are some examples of right and wrong punctuation, and pointers to help you get it right.

The apostrophe (')

The apostrophe is used mainly for three purposes:

1. To indicate one or more omitted letters (known as a *contraction*):

It's (*it is*) now your turn to ask the interviewer a question.

They're (*they are*) asking us for our references.

It'll (*it will*) take you 10 minutes to complete the application.

Don't (*do not*) ask about salary/benefits until the end of the interview.

2. To indicate the possessive case of nouns and pronouns, that is, possession of something:

I made the Dean's List.

Jon's business record is clearly outstanding.

The company's staff will be increased 12%.

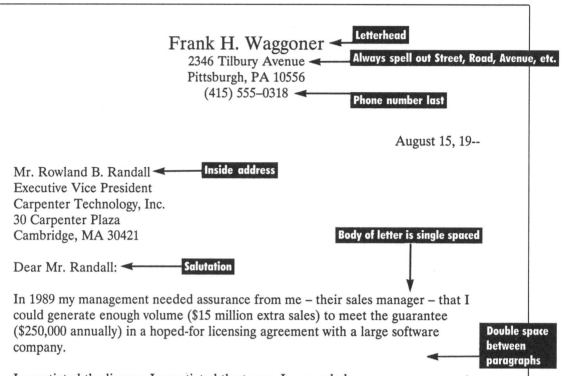

Frank H. Waggoner ← Letterhead
2346 Tilbury Avenue ← Always spell out Street, Road, Avenue, etc.
Pittsburgh, PA 10556
(415) 555–0318 ← Phone number last

August 15, 19--

Mr. Rowland B. Randall ← Inside address
Executive Vice President
Carpenter Technology, Inc.
30 Carpenter Plaza
Cambridge, MA 30421

Body of letter is single spaced

Dear Mr. Randall: ← Salutation

In 1989 my management needed assurance from me – their sales manager – that I could generate enough volume ($15 million extra sales) to meet the guarantee ($250,000 annually) in a hoped-for licensing agreement with a large software company.

Double space between paragraphs

I negotiated the license. I negotiated the terms. I persuaded my own management that I could deliver the sales, and told them of the possible profits. Then I led a team of 30 sales representatives in selling *over* $15 million worth of the new software product to computer stores throughout America. The guarantee was met, and on time.

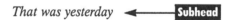
That was yesterday ← Subhead

What I am looking for now is a company poised and ready to break the CAD market wide open with the right sales leadership. I:

Double space before and after listings (if space permits)

– increased our sales per store / opened 150 new stores.
– increased our gross margin on sales.
– sold key accounts personally / opened Computerland with a $2.5 million order.
– and . . . gave us dramatically higher market penetration of the superstores.

The CAD market is growing far too fast, and is far too lucrative, to be left to a letter. I will call you shortly to arrange a meeting at a time convenient to you. Or, I may be reached at (415) 555–0318. Thank you.

Double space

Sincerely, ← Complimentary close

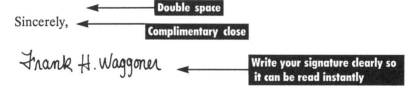
Write your signature clearly so it can be read instantly

3. To indicate the plurals of letters. (Recent changes in style rules have abolished the need for an apostrophe to show the plurals of numbers.)

There are two r's and two s's in the word embarrassed.

But:

As late as the 1950s, the accomplishment-oriented cover letter was not yet popular.

4. With people's names ending in *s*, add another *s* after the apostrophe to form the possessive:

Mrs. Williams's annual reviews of my performance were very fair.

When you want to indicate possession for a plural noun, add only the apostrophe:

Williams Brothers' prices are the lowest you will find.

These three companies' hiring policies are a model for the whole industry.

5. *Caution:* Don't use the apostrophe with possessive pronouns or to show possession with *it*:

This idea of theirs makes a lot of sense. *Not*: their's.

Hers is a job I would love to have. *Not*: her's.

The job is yours, if you still want it. *Not*: your's.

When the company makes its decision, all employees will be told. *Not*: it's.

Capitalization

There are many more rules for capitalizing letters than I intend to discuss here. First, you probably know most of them already, for example, the first word of every sentence is capitalized. Second, many of them will not come up in writing your cover letters.

We use capitals to designate a *specific* person, place or thing. For instance, the regions of the United States are *not* capitalized when they refer to points on the compass. They are capitalized when they refer to specific geographical areas:

The post office is located two blocks south, and one block west.

We drove east to the crossroads, and then drove north.

We planned to locate our new plant in the South, but later chose the Midwest.

The Southwest is the fastest growing economic region; the Northeast, the slowest.

We live in the Western hemisphere.

The seasons of the year are not capitalized:

I graduated in spring, 1992.

Our fall catalog comes out in August.

Our biggest selling season is summer.

Capitalize proper nouns (people, places and things):

the Hudson River / the Great Lakes / Atlantic Ocean

Reservations are where many Native Americans prefer to live.

The Chrysler Building is six blocks from Times Square.

I am starting my internship at St. Francis Hospital.

Labor Day is a rather old holiday; Martin Luther King Day is a relatively new one.

In the Great Depression, 30% of the work force was not working.

The Middle Ages and the Renaissance are subjects in her thesis.

In titles, capitalize every word except articles (a, an, the) and prepositions with fewer than four letters (of, in, etc.). Always capitalize the first word.

Charles Dickens wrote *A Tale of Two Cities*.

The titles of books and magazines are underlined or shown in italics.

How to Start, Expand and Sell a Business

How to Start, Expand and Sell a Business

Do not capitalize corporate titles, unless they are specific:

Ted is the best vice president of sales we've ever had.

Mr. Glenn is the company president, and Mr.

Klein is its chairperson.

We are advertising for a new controller.

Address the letter to James I. Port, Controller, and send a copy to Leonard A. Glasser, Vice President Manufacturing.

Capitalize titles other than corporate:

The Pope blessed the crowd in St. Peter's Square.

Officers recently promoted include Major Morgan and Captain Keen.

The department will never be the same without Professor Schuette.

The ecumenical service was conducted by Father Flynn and Rabbi Rosen.

Capitalize all trademarks, for example, Jello, Coke, Oreo, Kodak:

My favorite breakfast cereal is Wheaties.

Please Xerox 15 copies and give one to each of the staff.

I keep a box of Kleenex handy during hay fever season.

Capitalize the names of family members when you use them instead of their names:

When I needed help with my homework, I always turned to Father.

I said, "Oh, Grandmother, let me help you."

Capitalize other relatives only when you use them with the relative's name:

My Uncle Sam was invited, but could not come.

My uncle and my aunt were invited, but could not come.

Correct use of numbers

Numbers one through ten are written out. For numbers 11 and higher, polysyllables all, use the actual number. It is cumbersome to read *one hundred fifty* in place of *150*.

When you begin a sentence with a number, the number is written out:

Thirty years is the term of our lease.

Use a hyphen when combining numbers, and when combining a number with another word:

two 20-ton shipments / 45-person sales staff / a 200-dozen order

Thirty-five years ago, our company was founded.

Or rephrase the sentence:

Our company was founded 35 years ago.

As a matter of style, use *only* numerals in a sentence where one numeral is below ten, and another over:

I asked for 5 volunteers, and I got 15.

These come packed 2 to a carton, 12 cartons to a case.

Syllabication (dividing words at the ends of lines)

When there is not room at the end of a line to fit in a complete word, a hyphen (-) is used to indicate a word is divided. Divide a word only between syllables. For example, the word *in-ter-view* is composed of three syllables and can be divided at either of the hyphens shown. If you aren't certain how many syllables a word contains, consult your dictionary.

I would, however, counsel you not *to divide words at the ends of lines in your cover letters.* It is just one more tedious way to slow down the pace by making the reader work to reconnect the parts you have separated. The practice is unavoidable in books and periodicals set by machines, which must align right and left page margins perfectly. But your cover letters have an uneven right margin, permitting you to avoid hyphenating words. (Maybe the long word to be hyphenated should be replaced by a shorter word.)

None of the letters used as examples in this book has hyphenated words at the ends of lines. *Note*: Even if you use computer software that enables you to justify the right margin, it's a good idea not to. A jagged right margin breaks up the monotony of each line seeming exactly like every other one because all of them are precisely the same length.

Quotation marks (" ")

Quotation marks are used in pairs, one before and one after the material quoted. Placement of periods and commas when using a quotation are easy if you just remember this simple rule: All commas and periods go *within* the quotes (notice a comma or other punctuation mark precedes a quotation):

> Tom Jackson says in *The Hidden Job Market*, "Get in touch with the hidden job market."
> Jenny asked the interviewer, "When will you be making your decision?" and was told, "we still have a few more people to see."

Colons and semicolons are always placed *outside* quotation marks:

> "We'll let you know": This phrase is popular with interviewers whom you have failed to impress.

A question mark can come inside or outside the quotation marks, depending on the framework of the sentence:

> Where do you look to find "dream candidates"?
> My boss asked me, "Where do we look to find dream candidates?"

Abbreviations

An *abbreviation* is merely a shortened form of a word used in place of the complete word to save space and for convenience. The standard rule for abbreviations is to follow abbreviated words with a period, e.g., M.D., Dr., Mr., A.M., P.M., and so forth.

Always abbreviate well-known college degrees: B.S. rather than Bachelor of Science. M.B.A. rather than Master of Business Administration, M.A. rather than Master of Arts.

Abbreviate the names of the 50 states: Seattle, WA rather than Seattle, Washington. No period follows the state abbreviation.

When using *etc.* (the abbreviation for *et cetera*, used to indicate more of the same), it is always preceded and followed by a comma, unless it ends a sentence:

> I ordered copy paper, ball-point pens, paper clips, typewriter ribbons, etc., for our office.
> For our office I ordered copy paper, ball-point pens, paper clips, typewriters, etc.

Parenthetical abbreviations following names are preceded by a comma:

> John P. Jones, Jr. / William W. Wright, M.D. / Jennifer J. Wynett, C.P.A.

Exclamation Point (!)

Exclamation points are generally used to express astonishment or excitement. They should be used sparingly. (And use of multiple exclamation points —!!!— should be ruled out altogether.) Don't try to use the exclamation point to convince your reader something you've said is stirring, if the thought itself does not support it. Say what you have to say forcefully—and stop!

Summary

Accurate punctuation lends clarity to your cover letter and imparts a good impression of you as the employer scans through it. A carelessly drafted cover letter will present a poor impression of your competence to your prospective employer, and you may never be able to overcome the damage it has done to your job hopes.

CHAPTER 3

The Jump-Start Opening

The nine types of beginnings recommended in this chapter are supremely safe for you to use, and will propel any employer to immediately continue reading your cover letter.

You need never again stare at a blank sheet of paper trying to think of a compelling opening sentence. The only thing you need to remember is the same advice given to beginning newspaper reporters — *keep the lead short*.

Employers form snap judgments

Over and over again it must be repeated: The speed with which your cover letter must act to catch an employer's attention is measured in short, short seconds. Employers form snap judgments about you with your first sentence.

Don't just take my word for it. Carl Boll says, in *Executive Jobs Unlimited* (The Macmillan Company, 1965), "The first paragraph must catch the reader's interest instantly. It must make him sit up in his swivel chair; he must react as if you had rung his doorbell." And Richard Beatty says, in *The Perfect Cover Letter* (John Wiley & Sons, Inc., 1989), "The first paragraph can render the cover letter useless if it fails to compel sufficient interest on the part of the reader to warrant his/her further reading. It is important, therefore, to get your reader's attention right from the start by opening your letter in an interesting manner."

Boll says it and Beatty says it and now I am saying it: *Bore the reader at the start, and you've lost a prospective employer just like that!* (I just snapped my fingers.)

Realize 80% of job openings are *not* advertised; so 80% of the time, your letter is an uninvited caller. Employers do not consider it their duty to plow through all the unsolicited cover letters flowing to their desks asking for job interviews.

Remember, it is an introductory *sentence* — not a paragraph. Ordinarily, one sentence, sometimes two, no more than 15 to 20 words each, should do. The rule to keep in mind is this: Your first sentence or two must *force* a reading of the second paragraph. If your opening sentence could tell the employer your whole story, there would be no need for the rest of your letter. Apply the easy suggestions that follow, and the technique will come naturally.

Offer an immediate reader benefit

Open your cover letter with a reader benefit — an offer to solve a problem, or fulfill a wish — and you have an insurance policy guaranteeing your reader won't stop reading.

What subjects interest employers most? Themselves and their organizations. So your opening must show what you will do for the person and for the organization. There are only two questions running through any employer's mind: "Will I be safe hiring you?" and "What can you do to make me look good?" *Everything* you say that answers those two questions will be listened to carefully. Let's take a look at some openings that do:

By using intense training and pay-for-
    performance plans, I can virtually guarantee

to bring down the cost you are now paying to perform any messaging task.

Here is an idea you can put to work immediately to increase the efficiency of your operations.

I am an accountant who earns his cost back. By the end of the first year, I will save the company money in one way or another.

One of the things you can't fail to notice in my resume is my unrelenting campaign to (1) slash time-consuming paper work, and (2) eliminate nonessential steps.

If you have been wrestling with the problem of how to build your agency's profits in this recessionary market, my resume will hold interest for you.

You can place business without having to go to a wholesaler.

You can open yourself up to new markets, virtually overnight.

A whole army of top-earning designers are going to work to make you rich, but you are going to add only *one* designer's salary to your payroll.

Ask a question

Open with a question—particularly one asked directly of the employer. A question so relevant or challenging as to grab the employer's curiosity at once and impel further reading to find the answer.

When you use a question as an opener, you must be sure it is the kind of question that will start only one train of thought in the mind of your target— *and will lead only to the conclusion you want reached.*

Make sure, also, the answer to your opening question is thought out carefully and is credible. Your reader must not be allowed to feel deceived after being led into the body of your letter by a curiosity-arousing question, or you will be dropped in disgust. Begin at once to follow through on the reward-for-reading commitment you make in your question. Remember your reader will not continue unless your second paragraph fulfills the expectation aroused by your question:

How good a judge are you of how much reward is needed to inspire above-average sales results?

What do you do when overnight you find your own firm acquired by a larger broker, and twice the number of brokers are now going after the same accounts?

In these rather bleak times in real estate, you may be asking yourself, "Where and how and by what means am I going to make more money from the property I own?"

Do you want to sell J. Crew's future?

Are you getting all the new accounts you deserve? Would you like to take an enormous jump?

Are you enjoying all the profits from the Middle East you could be?

Would you like to get a toehold in Europe to be ready for future profits? Someone like myself could make all the difference.

How much are rising maintenance and renovation costs hurting your profits?

Mention a personal referral

One of the best, if not *the* best beginning, is the *referral* opening. It links you to the employer at once by dropping the name of someone whose name the employer recognizes and, in many cases, admires, who feels the employer would benefit by hiring you. The employer's curiosity about why you are being recommended impels further reading.

In the April 10, 1992, issue of *National Business Employment Weekly*, in an article titled "How to Get Noticed by an Executive Recruiter," writer Perri Capell says, "Write, don't call . . . search consultants will almost always talk with or meet a candidate referred by a colleague, friend, client or candidate they have placed previously."

When such personal contacts are known to you, by all means profit from them. Then, when your letter is pulled from its envelope, you are no longer a total stranger. Suggestion: The next time someone suggests a person you can contact about a job, ask, "Why do you feel I would be right for them?" You may get an approving comment you can quote in your opening that will make the employer take more serious notice of you:

> I met Paul Vinorese at the Automobile Show in Dallas, and he suggested I contact you. Mark Showalter, of GMAC, also suggested I contact you, as he felt, "you would be perfect for their company."

> Mickey Hart, Couture Buyer of Bonwit Teller, who has observed my work here at Bonwit's, suggested—recommended—I write to you about a sales position in your new sportswear division.

Refer to the employer's ad

No discussion of cover letter openings is complete without mentioning the most commonly used beginning of them all: referring to the employer's newspaper recruitment ad. Forty-nine out of fifty cover letters using this approach start this way:

> I am responding to your ad in the *Cincinnati Enquirer*, March 7, 1992, for a (title of position).

> Better:

> Several things you said in your ad for a (title of position) suggest you may be searching for someone with my background.

> Or:

> One of the things that interested me when I read your ad for a (title of position) was your emphasis on . . .

You provide yourself with a handy device for swiftly matching your own accomplishments to the requirements of the ad. *Note*: It isn't necessary to mention the newspaper's name or the date the ad appeared. Employers key their ads, i.e., they use codes such as "Box NT," "Attn: T. Richards," etc., in the return address to tell them which ad you are responding to. Here are three more examples, with a slight twist:

> You'll notice quickly my resume meets six of the seven requirements in your ad for a Director of Manufacturing. I reserved the seventh to mention here.

> I believe I am truly well qualified for the position of Music Marketing Assistant, without being overqualified. In fact, it is precisely the position I am seeking.

> Several things you said in your ad for a Customer Service Representative lead me to feel you are looking for someone with my philosophy about service.

Refer to news about the employer

Use this opening *when there is a plausible connection between the news item and your own story:*

> Congratulations on Pepsi's megabillion barter arrangement with the Soviet Union.

> Bravo! on your acquiring the Modern Miss 76-store chain, and on your ambitious plans for future growth, as mentioned in today's *Women's Wear Daily*.

> Congratulations on your acquisition of the TCBY account. Not too long ago people congratulated *me* for setting up a co-op ad program for TCBY that met all the needs of their franchisees—and increased their market share.

Use offbeat statements or fascinating facts that arouse curiosity

The technique here is simple: You hold back information briefly to arouse curiosity, and the reader dutifully reads on:

> Autopsies seldom benefit those upon whom they are performed. Except when you are examining dormant accounts.

> Here's a fact from *The Wall Street Journal* you perhaps don't know: A lost customer cuts company profits by $175, contrasted with the $30 it takes to keep a customer satisfied.

> If we had numbers for names, mine would be 12. In any museum (except the Smithsonian), they

would place someone like me in a glass case without a moment's hesitation and label it "Extinct Species."

Here is your own continuous, unlimited source of greater sales from unexpected places — *me*.

You perhaps do not know me, but I know you because I call you every day, and sometimes more often.

You'll generally find only one person like me in any company. I'm the sales rep that ranks No. 1 in virtually every category.

Use a quotation

Use any quotation that fits both your own story and the interests of the employer you want to reach. There *must be* a plausible connection. The employer must never be allowed to feel fooled while being lead from the opening quotation into your second paragraph. (See Chapter 7.) I like to use quotations for openings. They loosen up your writing and give it a personal touch, especially if you are writing about dry facts:

Baron Rothschild, the famous 19th-century banker, was supposed to have said, "I would not give five minutes listening to someone tell me how to make $1 million, but I would stay up all night listening to how I could keep from losing $100,000."

You've heard the expression, "A salesperson is only as strong as their line," which means the real sales burden falls on the shoulders of designers like me.

Write a headline

Here's still another manner of starting — a most unusual and unexpected eye-catcher — but it's a little tricky. Get your reader interested by stating a benefit you offer that is startling *and present it in the form of a headline*. You have to make a special effort to find the striking benefit, and then to phrase it with tight economy of words. But if you do, it's an excellent way to start. For instance:

The man who has made more millions for his

company in the tour business than they ever dreamed possible can help you make money, too.

You know — we all know — headlines have been used to flag attention since newspapers were invented. They can be adapted to impart a feeling of increased self-confidence to your cover letter. A business writing consultant told me:

I've polled personnel managers and know they respond favorably to creative openers that set the tone of the letter. Sometimes the opening tells more about the applicant than the rest of the letter.

State your job objective

Another well-liked beginning, for its directness and simplicity, is to state your job objective in your very first sentence:

I am writing you to explore employment opportunities as a quantitative analyst with IBM.

I am seeking a sales position with a women's large-size manufacturer where my product development ideas will help you tap this vastly underdeveloped market.

I respectfully ask the CIA to take into consideration my application for employment as a language professional in Serbo-Croatian.

You may be in need of a young man with my background for an entry-level position in Cablevision's data processing operations.

Summary

I have been extremely thorough in discussing the beginning of your cover letter because it is so fundamental. In order to tell an employer about yourself and your virtues, you must first grab attention. Your opening should stop readers like a skillfully written newspaper headline for a mass-circulation tabloid, and this is the way to do it. Employers like getting information in this style. Try it. The potential rewards far surpass any possible risks.

CHAPTER 4

Action Close

A strong close to your cover letter is just as basic as a strong beginning. You want the employer to spring from mere attention to practical action. In your final sentence you can clearly spell out the action you want the employer to take. But how many cover letters end as though the writer wants and expects traceable results?

How you close your letter says a lot about you

When you fail to close self-assuredly, it suggests to employers that you're cowed by their authority, by their terrible power to hire you or brush you off without so much as a sigh or a backward glance. You see the employer as the final arbiter. Right or wrong, there are no appeals by people in your position from an employer's snap judgments.

For many jobhunters, that is the whole story. Here are some earnest but trembling examples of closes from actual letters (italics mine) that reflect the average jobhunter's customary awe of the employer as an authority figure:

I would welcome the opportunity to meet with you *if* an opening exists for an accountant with my qualifications.

I sincerely *hope* you will give me the opportunity to meet with you and discuss the possibility of employment.

Thanking you very kindly, and *hoping* to hear from you in the near future.

Should my qualifications be of interest, I would welcome the opportunity to meet with you.

I would appreciate an opportunity to discuss *any* possible position that you may have in your organization.

If and *hope* are cautious words. They do not encourage action. They imply doubt, invite hesitation, and all in all are a low-spirited way to ask for a response. You display a lack of confidence in how the reader is going to react to what you've just written: You *hope* the reader is impressed. Hope is a start. Why not take action to support your hope? When you weaken at the close, you confer dependency status on yourself. Realize we all want to be loved, but the business world has no plan for becoming our lover. The strongest message you can send to any employer is "I don't need you." (See examples among the 100 letters.)

I have deliberately labored the point here because it is one you ought to be aware of—don't humble yourself at the close. However, it is a very easily corrected fault, which I am going to show you how to remedy right here and now. When the late Sam Walton, founder of Wal-mart stores, was asked the secret of his success, he said, "High expectations are the key to everything."

What kind of action should we ask for?

Make your close work for you. When the employer's identity is known to you, close your letter by saying *you will call the employer next week*. There's no way an employer can get unhappy with you for asking for an interview.

You must believe deeply, firmly and sincerely that what you offer is in the best interests of the employer you are trying to persuade to invite you in for an employment interview. If you believe this way, you can sincerely pull for your employer to summon you for the employer's own benefit.

It has been convincingly proven that a salesperson's *expectancy* has a direct bearing on the prospect's decision. Expect a positive response from every letter you send to a job you are right for. *Write the close before you start.* At the time you are writing your opening, you know what the last line will say. Close with a confident, positive request for a meeting.

By way of emphasizing this even further, if you do not honestly feel employers are the losers if they do not at least meet you, then maybe you ought to put this book on the shelf for a while until you start believing in yourself and taking pride in your work history. Believe in yourself and your abilities and you will transfer that belief to the employer.

How to overcome your fear of rejection

You will notice not all the cover letters used as examples in this book (apart from those addressed to P.O. Box numbers) close with a pledge to phone the employer to arrange an interview. There is a reason for that.

These jobhunters do not wish to risk the possibility of rejection, of being made to feel unwanted. There is a fine French proverb that describes their state of mind: *le mieux est l'ennemi du bien* (leave well enough alone). Besides, lots of people still do get interviews despite their sitting still and waiting for the employer to take the initiative and call them.

Fear of rejection by employers is a big (and unjustified) fear among jobhunters. It is the single biggest obstacle to your getting jobs you are right for. You fear rejection because you feel you are doing something *to* the employer (a perfect stranger). Whereas you must believe you are doing something

for the employer. L.E. Frailey says, as he so excellently says almost everything in his monumental book (over 900 pages) *Handbook of Business Letters* (Prentice Hall, 1948): "There is no reason why any individual should have a feeling of inferiority or dread in asking for a job. The person who reads the letter is a buyer of work hours; the person who writes it has work hours for sale."

Follow up your letter with a phone call

I won't listen to you say that calling an employer about a job is not in you, or you can't. If you want a fat bank account, winter vacations in the Caribbean, and not having to look at price tags, then you will take the phone in hand to support every letter you write (where the employer is known to you).

Even if you are not now working and are prey to all the anxieties that torment a person out of a job, you must be willing to do things in your job search that initially make you uncomfortable or a little scared. Just as you have learned to live with a dread of an employer's rejection, you can also learn to live without it.

Realize all self-confidence is *acquired*; none of us is born with self-confidence. Those friends and fellow workers all of us know, who seem to be poised and ready with assured, thoughtful responses to any and all situations, *acquired* their poise and confidence. And you can, too. You can duplicate the success of anyone you admire. The attempt is worth the trial, if you do not desire to live as you are now compelled to live.

When you beat back your fears of calling employers, you will often open doors to opportunities you thought were locked tight.

Employers are not in a hurry to act as we'd like them to

Here's still another reason for the action close. Often an employer is impressed with your letter but doesn't take any action because there is no urgency to act. Adding staff to the payroll (or reducing) is a responsibility most executives are not in a hurry to deal with.

Not-in-a-hurry is one of the toughest obstacles for jobhunters to conquer. The employer agrees you look impressive on paper but is not moved to act.

Realize that interviewing and hiring people is one of the functions executives least like to do. Oh, yes! There is too much room for misjudgment, as I mention in Chapter 6. Managers prefer to leave at least the initial screening to personnel, an employment agency or an executive recruiter.

That's why your power-packed words must propel the employer, or any other reader, to the point of action. You provide two choices: Pick up the phone and call me, or I will call you. There is no third choice.

Employers carry *No!* on their tongues, so why not rid your letters of any obstacle that makes it harder or less handy for the employer to meet you face to face?

I know the phone can weigh a ton when you're out of work and standing in line for unemployment. All the same, you *will* enhance the likelihood of your being invited in for an interview if you call the employer, rather than wait for the employer to call you.

Perhaps you think that such assertiveness may be resented. Leave that wrong idea here. The employer knows what you want. Ask for it. Employers are perfectly free to do as they please about granting your request.

Take your cue from sales letters

All sales letters close with a sentence telling the reader exactly what is expected: *Place an order now.* It might be useful here to give a few examples of the forceful, bold closes that are standard in all good sales letters, because that is what a cover letter is.

Here are some closing sentences from sales letters selected at random. Notice how all of these letters end by firmly asking you to take action, without hedging, flinching or cringing.

From Publisher's Clearing House

"Remember, one entry makes you eligible for all prizes in this bulletin, so be sure to enter by January 24."

Full-page ad by a book publisher

"With the fantastic contents that are certain to help you earn additional spare time income in your own unique business, why wait? Mail your order today with your check or money order for only $9.99."

Subscription sales letter from Advertising Age

"To get your free 10-issue subscription to *Advertising Age* all you need do is sign and return the enclosed Acceptance Certificate. Simply mail your Acceptance Certificate in the postage-paid envelope provided. Please respond by no later than the free offer deadline date of 5/26/92."

Thank-you letter from National Multiple Sclerosis Society

Not-for-profit organizations know the way to raise money to support their activities is to *ask* for money—firmly enough, and often enough. Here's part of the text on a card sent to thank me for my past support:

> "Every hour . . . every day . . . multiple sclerosis strikes a young adult. Yes, I want to help my neighbors with MS. Here is my tax-deductible contribution of: (   )$100 (   )$50 (   )$20 (   )Other $_____."

You will find most response coupons at the bottom of ads regularly take the liberty of putting words in your mouth, e.g., "Yes! Send me a copy of *How Mail Order Fortunes Are Made.* I enclose $15. . . ." Another: "Yes! Send my copy of *The New Social Security Guide* at once. Enclosed is my $9.95."

Anyone who has ever clipped a coupon and donated money, or ordered merchandise or a service from an ad, knows how inoffensive such language is when you find you *want* the product or service being offered.

The complimentary close

Sincerely, followed by a comma, is known as a *complimentary close*. Probably three-quarters of business letters end with the word *Sincerely*. I find it very serviceable. The other 25% is composed of phrases such as *Sincerely yours, Yours very truly*, and so forth. There's no harm in your using them; there's no point in it either. Why use two or three words to express what can be said in one? Your cover letter can be used to cultivate an image of someone who says things in as few words as possible.

"Thank you"

The last two words of every cover letter I have ever written are *thank you*. I wish to express my gratitude to the employer for taking the time to read my letter. The following sections give fourteen closes that strive to put readers in a frame of mind to take the next step:

Because you've read this far, then you must have an interest in how to cut food and beverage costs. I intend to call you next week and arrange a convenient time to meet. Or, I may be reached at (718) 555–7745. Thank you.

I know this time of year finds you very busy. I would be reluctant to seek an interview with you now if I did not feel I can have a marked influence on your fall business. I will call you next week to arrange a day and time convenient for us to meet. Thank you.

Just give me the chance to convince you in an interview. I will prove a helpful aide, and a year from now you will congratulate yourself (and me). Thank you.

There is too much stored profit potential in knockoffs, at least to me, to be left to a letter. You are now getting into your spring selling season, so I will call you next week to arrange a convenient time for us to meet. Or, I may be reached at (718) 555–7745. Thank you.

The right moves can give your sales overwhelming force in this region. Let us work together to bring this about. For your convenience, I will call you to arrange an interview. Or, I may be reached at (718) 555–7745. Thank you.

I would like to meet with you and give you some more of the dozens of examples I have of how tough-willed cold calling opens new accounts. I will call you next week to arrange an interview. Or, I may be reached at (718) 555–7745. Thank you.

It's fun trying to cut costs to rock bottom and become the low-cost operator. If you like that kind of fun, too, let's talk. I will call you next week to arrange a convenient time for us to meet in your office. Or, I may be reached at (718) 555–7745. Thank you.

Even, if in the end, it is not in the cards that we work together, I believe you still will wish to hear my ideas on assuring *perfect* quality in finished garments. I will contact you in a few days to arrange a mutually convenient time for us to meet. Or, I may be reached at (718) 555–7745. Thank you.

The best I can hope to do in this letter is to acquaint you with myself and let you know my strong interest in this position. When will it be agreeable with you for the two of us to meet? I'll call you next Wednesday. Thank you.

Closes that state the applicant's objective

What I am seeking is a large, stable domestic mill or converter that wishes to break the mass-merchandiser market wide open. I will call you next week to arrange a convenient time for us to meet. Or, I may be reached at (718) 555–7745. Thank you.

I am seeking a sales position where I can set

more records and make more money. Just give me the chance to convince you in an interview. I'll call you next week, or I may be reached at (718) 555–7745. Thank you.

What I am seeking now is a management position with a retail grocery or wholesaler where I can use my experience to motivate workers and build sales.

I am seeking to manage a much larger facility because I like the tempo, and I know I can handle it to your complete satisfaction.

Close for use in responding to a P. O. Box number

If you are responding to an employment ad that does not give the employer's name and address, e.g., a post office, newspaper or other box number, then this close is appropriate:

I am a thoroughgoing sales professional, both in cold calling for new accounts, and in breathing life into dormant accounts. Give me the opportunity to convince you in a personal interview. *Because I cannot call you, I may be reached at (718) 555–7745.* Thank you.

This close implies to the employer you would prefer to act — to pick up the phone and call, if only you could.

Summary

My counsel to you in this chapter is simple: You absolutely cannot go wrong asking an employer for an interview in your cover letter. This is a skill you can easily master from examples given. Stick to the idea that you are requesting an interview because it's in the employer's best interest, and your own, and you can't go wrong. Employers admire self-confident applicants.

CHAPTER 5

Common Mistakes That Hold Cover Letter Writers Back . . .
And What To Do About Them

This chapter will help you to spot and avoid common cover letter mistakes that make employers yawn. Because holding the employer's interest longer has so much bearing on whether you get interviews, we are now going to review ways to do it.

Mention specific accomplishments

Accomplishments are the single most important element of every cover letter, and one that is overlooked remarkably often. Failure to list measurable accomplishments of specific interest to the reader is a major reason why cover letters are passed over by employers. You will find a thorough discussion of accomplishments in Chapter 6.

Don't repeat accomplishments given in your resume

In the November 15, 1991 issue of *National Business Employment Weekly*, Jane K. Cleland, C.E.O. of a marketing firm, critiques the over 250 resumes and cover letters she received from an ad the firm had run for an administrative assistant: "Almost every resume was boring. And the attached letters typically reiterated the stuff already covered in the resume."

The answer to this problem is simple. Merely reserve one or two of your peak accomplishments for the cover letter, and save the rest for your resume.

Don't be excessively courteous

"Ah, be very humble now, very humble indeed. Tell us what it is you require. Tell it quickly, nervously and without a vestige of self-respect. If no trouble to us in any way, we'll see what we can do."

　　—*Sister Carrie*, Theodore Dreiser

Most cover letter writers, particularly recent graduates with little work experience, seem as ill at ease in their cover letters as a man appearing in a tuxedo for the first time. Great formality and excessive courtesy are hallmarks of insecurity.

The inclination of many of us who lead conservative lives is to be still more conservative in addressing employers, often to the point of appearing meek, submissive or even needy. Just the opposite is required. Your cover letter is far more likely to move an employer by being uncommonly bold and self-confident.

Don't focus on your own wants and needs instead of the employer's

A prevalent fault among many cover letters is that they are written from the jobhunter's point of view. I think this is the single biggest failing with most of the cover letters reaching my desk. They have no fundamental interest except to the jobseekers who wrote them. And this the busy employer will never forgive.

If those who are on the reading end of cover letters are in agreement on any one point, it is this one. I quote from "Letters to the Personnel Department" (*Handbook of Business Letters*, Prentice Hall, 1948): "Any businessman who handles application letters knows how much they follow the same old groove. They follow a monotonous description of personal characteristics."

Don't give your work phone number in your cover letter

It makes you seem too available. Employers are frightened by job applicants who appear needy or desperate. And the employer wonders why you would jeopardize your present position by receiving calls from other employers at work.

Realize employers are accustomed to calling jobhunters at home, after work hours, where an unhurried conversation can be held. List *only* your home phone in your cover letter.

Don't misspell words, particularly the employer's or the company's name

Correct spelling and proper punctuation are not only in good taste, they are mandatory. The use of misspelled words and the misuse of punctuation marks, when correct spelling and punctuation is expected, does not inspire confidence in an employer.

Don't give "salary history" or "salary requirements"

You stand an excellent chance of hanging yourself by disclosing your salary history and expectations in your cover letter. And because jobseekers do not ordinarily hang themselves for pleasure, salary is a topic you should avoid discussing in your cover letter.

Some examples of poorly written cover letters

There is no Pulitzer Prize awarded for writing cover letters. Perhaps there ought to be one awarded to employers for reading them. On pages 24-27 I have reprinted four cover letters jobhunters brought to me for evaluation and rewriting.

After reading them, you perhaps may think I have gone out of my way to select only the poorest examples for more profound contrast with the examples given in this book. I assure you such is not the case. These letters are fairly typical. If I wished to select the worst examples, I would have included examples such as the one on the facing page, and even this one is not rare.

You will see that all of these letters have multiple weaknesses that bring yawns from employers. The point I want to stress in showing you these letters is *write for the employer and not for yourself*, and you will be listened to.

Summary

This chapter is about avoiding common mistakes that can torpedo your cover letter's chances almost before the ink on it is dry. Actually, the rules of writing effective cover letters are quite simple. You can learn them once and for all right here in this book. If, after finishing this book, your cover letter does not bring you the hoped-for interview for some job you had your sights on (if I may say so strange a thing), you will at least know it was not because you wrote a bad letter. There is a lot of competition. Last year, 13,206 high school graduates competed to enter Stanford University's freshman class of 1,580. Among the applicants were over 2,600 with perfect 4.0 (A) averages.

All-Purpose

William H. Krauss
29 Pine Hollow Road
Boston, MA 12055
(402) 555–1745

To whom it may concern:

I would be interested in any new career opportunity that would motivate, challenge and financially reward me. I want to contribute my skills, talents and intelligence and receive respect and acknowledgment for my time and work.

I will bring to you the following: charisma, creativity, organization, ingenuity, foresight, modern, fashionable, sensitive, compassionate, assertive, sports-minded, cultured, liberal, liberated, old-fashioned, artistic, analytical, etc.

I have been out of work since March, 1990. The first 5 months I chose to relax and most recently have searched many different fields of interest. I did temp work and per diem odd jobs to earn money. I'm looking for the right niche to keep me smiling, energetic and rich. Can we talk?

Sincerely,

Weaknesses
- **Focuses almost exclusively on the writer's own wants** — six of the eight sentences start with *I*.
- **Mentions being out of work** — a topic best avoided in cover letters.
- **No mention of specific accomplishments** — the most important element in a cover letter.
- **States the obvious** — "I did temp work and per diem odd jobs *to earn money*," which makes the writer appear dumb.

Kenneth H. Braun, Jr.
44 E. Madison Court
Chicago, IL 30368
(302) 555–0124

Dear Human Resources Director:

Enclosed is a copy of my resume in application for an entry-level position with your company. As a Business Administration graduate of the University of Miami with some experience in business, I believe that my skills would be well suited to your company.

I can offer you a strong desire and determination to succeed coupled with an ability to learn quickly. If you will give me the opportunity to prove myself, I can guarantee you that I will develop rapidly for you.

Please carefully review my qualifications and contact me, at your convenience, if you would like me to come in for an interview. I would welcome the opportunity to come and speak with you. Thank you for your time and consideration, and I look forward to hearing from you soon.

Sincerely,

Weaknesses
- **Salutation**—Words after Dear should be lowercase, e.g., human resources director.
- **Stating the obvious**—"Enclosed is a copy of my resume. . . ."
- **Weak close**—"Contact me, at your convenience, if you would like me to come in for an interview." Writer places himself in dependency status.
- **No mention of specific accomplishments**
- **No mention of the position being applied for**

Operations Manager

Sander M. Bettelman
49 Dogwood Drive
Allentown, PA 10005
Home: (215) 555–1436
Work: (215) 555–2231

Dear Mr. McTeague:

The position of Divisional Operations Executive is of interest to me.

As a senior executive with over 20 years of diversified overall responsibility for accounting, financial planning, capital expenditures, financing and treasury with exposure to acquisitions, mainly overseas and international areas.

As an international financial and operational executive with past exposure; including working 2 years in the Far East, 5 years in Europe, and 4 years in South America. My current position is in the financial and operational areas for the past 5 years.

I have hands-on heavy corporate experience in the designing, installing and system development in IBM and Digital Equipment. My development in data processing includes financial, operational and administrative and marketing. My current compensation is $145,000 and profit sharing. However, starting compensation is negotiable.

Sincerely yours,

Weaknesses
- **Bland, self-focused opening** — "The position of Divisional Operations Executive is of interest to *me*."
- **Long, long sentences tire the reader** — Second paragraph is composed of a single sentence fragment of 30 words, followed by one of 28 words.
- **First sentence of third paragraph is grammatically incorrect**
- **No mention of specific accomplishments**
- **Mentions current salary**
- **Gives phone number at work**

Robert A. Taylor
1073 Fanny Street
Princeton, NJ 12401
(201) 555–1661

Gentlemen:

I am seeking a position in the machine tool industry, preferably in the production area, where my experience is at its utmost, where I can contribute my knowledge, motivation, reliability and have maximum growth potential.

As you review my resume, you will find my experience has developed and expanded in many areas of the machine tool industry. I am willing to start where my experience is most suitable to demonstrate my competence, and progress according to my ability.

If there is an appropriate opening in your company, I would enjoy a personal meeting to further express my qualifications. Your reply will be appreciated.

Sincerely,

Weaknesses
- **Sexist salutation ("Gentlemen")** — old-fashioned and now offensive.
- **Tedious opening** — a single sentence of 35 words (twice the average length recommended).
- **Focuses on own needs rather than employer's**
- **No mention of specific accomplishments**
- **Passive close** — starts with *if*, a word not calculated to impel action.

Computer Programmer

Mildred M. Keesler
21 Laurelton Turnpike
Atlanta, GA 12411
(404) 555–7864

Gentlemen:

Enclosed please find my resume for your review and evaluation. As you can see from the attached resume, my employment background has been primarily in the area of mainframes. I have also had three weeks of formal training in the use of Nixdorf computers. However, if you find that my skills can be put to effective use elsewhere in your organization, I would appreciate your consideration and notification of the appropriate position.

I feel confident that if given the opportunity, I could benefit your organization by providing the experience I possess. I would appreciate a personal interview to discuss a position for which I am qualified. I look forward to hearing from you in the near future.

Again, thank you for your consideration.

Sincerely,

Weaknesses
- **Sexist opening** — and old-fashioned.
- **Long-winded opening** — seven lines (when a maximum of three is recommended) / leads the reader to refer to the resume instead of drawing the reader into the body of the letter.
- **Excessively polite** — last three sentences make the writer appear obsequious.
- **No mention of specific accomplishments**

CHAPTER 6

Lessons From Advertising

What I hope to do in this chapter is to pass on to you some principles and practical tips the advertising experts use to impel complete reading of ads and immediate purchase of the advertised product or service. You will be interested in how readily adaptable these concepts are to getting responses from your own cover letters.

Hiring decisions are as much emotional as logical

Before we go further, let's go back to 1938, and review the words of Dr. Karl A. Menninger, founder of the Menninger Clinic (*Man Against Himself*, Harcourt Brace, 1938; now in its 20th printing), to gain perspective and focus:

> "We all know by now that conscious motives cannot be relied upon to explain human behavior. There are too many instances where the motives are not to the slightest degree recognized by the person himself."

An employer's heart dictates to the brain

An employer's decision to hire you is based on feeling and emotion, as much as on facts and logic. If you remember only this single point, you will have learned a very good thing from this chapter. Pascal, French philosopher and mathematician, said, "The heart has its reasons with which reason is unacquainted." And Freud told us, "When emotion and intellect come into conflict, emotion always wins."

Pascal made his observation in the 17th century; Freud made his in the 19th century. It has not changed since.

Every corporate manager with hiring authority has subconscious psychological needs and desires that dominate every hiring decision—needs and desires the skilled cover letter writer will attempt to fill. At the top of the list is *security—a need to stay safe. Fear* is one of the emotions that governs the actions of every human being. Next is *prestige—a desire to look good*. Here are some others: A desire for promotion and more money. A desire for more power. A desire for less worry and less work.

Employers need to stay safe and secure

In the executive life, everybody watches for everyone else's blunders, and everyone attempts to associate with people who'll do them credit.

The boss wants to rise in the organization, and must, therefore, be assured that hiring you presents no source of future embarrassment that could reveal poor hiring judgment. Suppose someone the boss hired becomes a laughingstock, the butt of office gossip because of a previously undetected quirk. Office gossip: "Did you hear what he did at the managers' meeting yesterday?" "No, tell me." The boss is faced with a predicament. Retention is embarrassing, firing is costly and awkward, and then there is the matter of a replacement. Another mistake . . . and a long-hoped-for promotion might slip away.

The boss fears making a hiring mistake that could be frowned on by those in a position to influence the boss's future course in that organization. The cover letter writer who demonstrates that the prospective boss runs no risk whatever in hiring the applicant will relieve this fear and stand a good chance of hearing from the boss.

Employers hope you will make them look good

The boss has a second emotional need to be filled in hiring you—the need to look good. All of us, when we select our clothes, have an eye out for what will make us look good. The same in hiring. The boss looks for job applicants who will do *the boss* credit: higher productivity, brighter, livelier, gets along with everybody, does more than is expected, shining past accomplishments. In short, the type about whom your colleagues and superiors will ask, "Jenny's a wonder woman; where do you find people like that all the time?"

Enter the world of the accomplishment. Employers pay more attention to accomplishments than to almost anything else in your cover letter.

Accomplishments

Accomplishments are ideas, procedures, policies, products, decisions and so forth you have either introduced or taken a leading role in that contributed to building the organization bigger and better.

Your past achievements are the single most important factor of all

You are hired, promoted and rewarded on the basis of your accomplishments, so you can lay them on with a trowel in your cover letter. Your readers will love you for it. Even an improperly written cover letter will gain you interviews if it is brimming with profit-aiding accomplishments.

Accomplishments show you've already performed with distinction. If the accomplishments in your cover letter are specific to the work you are applying for, then the boss begins to feel there is

minimum risk in hiring you, and a growing feeling you could make the boss look good.

Your accomplishments make bosses flush with pride

In this respect, bosses are not unlike proud parents who are congratulated for the star performance of a son or daughter. Bosses are convinced your past achievements are the best forecaster of your future success.

Prospective bosses, therefore, need accomplishments as grounds for choosing you, or as excuses to show that hiring you is safe and wise, and to vindicate their decision to higher-ups if they are later questioned or criticized. They need to justify to themselves a hiring judgment that is based as much on emotion as on logic and deductive reasoning. In a manual written to train executives in interviewing techniques, the author warns executives to watch out for the biggest executive hiring mistake: *hiring in your own image.*

This surface desire to find the fittest candidate and look good (and the nagging subconscious fear of *making a mistake that could come back to haunt you*) is the reason for getting the opinion of others. Enter the multiple corporate interview (plus testing, the services of the executive recruiter, the employment agency, the human resources people, etc.). In a survey I conducted of 500 employers in 1985, I asked the question, "Do you ever consult anyone else in making hiring decisions?" Ninety-five percent said, "Yes."

One young woman told me she had gone through six interviews at one organization for the position of secretary. A young, aspiring stockbroker told me he went one morning for an interview to a famous broker, and expected to spend only an hour or two—he spent eight. Every one of you who has experienced multiple employment interviews knows exactly what I am talking about.

Underpinning it all (on the employer's side) is the fear of making a hiring error. This explains, also, why hiring people is one of the tasks managers least like to perform.

Therefore, the more credible accomplishments and benefits you pile on, the more sound reasons you give to prop up the employer's already-made decision to hire you. This is such an important point that it might be well to emphasize it by asking you to endure still another quote: Philosopher and psychologist William James said, "Our reason is quite satisfactory, in 999 cases out of 1,000, if it can find a few arguments that will do to recite in case our credulity is criticized by someone else."

Duties vs. accomplishments

Listing mere duties performed without telling how *well* they were performed, or the benefit that accrued to the employer by reason of their performance, is a principal reason cover letters and resumes are passed over by employers.

Let me try to make my point with a little illustration. Suppose you ran a help-wanted ad seeking a secretary and got 100 responses that all said, "I type and take dictation. I file. I answer the phone and take messages, greet visitors, make appointments, order supplies, and so on." How long would you go on reading before you started skimming pages at a rate of 10 to 20 seconds a page? The responses seem as much alike as an office full of secretaries all dressed in white satin dresses or suits. This is the reason cover letters and resumes are given glance-and-run treatment by prospective employers. But suppose you said:

- I type 95 w.p.m., and get out letters 25% faster than others in our office, leaving me more time to take on new duties.
- I found a new vendor for our supplies, 5–20% cheaper on office staples than the supplier our company had used for 15 years.
- I often handle two, even three, phone conversations at once when we get busy, without seeming harried, hasty or discourteous.
- I missed only one day in two years, and have never been late.

I could go on, but I think you get the point. It's pointing out the superior manner in which you carry out required office tasks that gives you an advantage over your competitors for the job opening, and lead to your cover letter being read fully. So much for the theory behind the need to state your duties in the form of accomplishments. From this point on we are going to get down to the ways of doing it.

The accomplishments most noticed

The most favorably noticed accomplishments are the ones that make *a direct, identifiable contribution to the organization's profits*. Here are three nice examples:

One coupon promotion was so successful, it increased gross sales on the products involved 2% (ordinarily, discount promotions lose revenue).

After one year in charge, I increased annual sales to $1.2 million (with profit increase of 16%).

Started office deliveries: delivery service has gone from zero to present $750 a week.

Your cover letter will stand out from the competition if you merely emphasize you are profit *conscious*. Boll says in *Executive Jobs Unlimited*:

An employer is interested in anything that will lead to the conservation of time or money; the speeding of production; new ideas or methods to improve the qualities of his products; policies that will lead to smoother employee relations; anything that adds to the smooth running of the business, to its more successful operation, also adds to the profit picture.

Let's look at some examples of accomplishments from letters in this book:

I increased production from 60 doz. blouses a day to 120 doz. by demonstrating to each of the 140 employees how to do their jobs more efficiently.

I designed my own employee training program that was later adopted by corporate management as the standard for all franchises.

You will see in my resume I placed people in the hundreds, and that 90% of them are still in their jobs as I write this.

My work made it possible for NYNEX to cut its run time by 50%, enabling a 70% reduction in staffing needs.

A miscalculation by me could lose forever sales NBC might have had, or forced them to buy back the oversold time at a loss of up to $25,000.

Don't mention identical accomplishments in resume and cover letter. Cover letter writers need repeated admonitions not to use the same accomplishments in the cover letter that the reader is going to see in your resume in a few moments. I mentioned this in Chapter 2, but it's worth repeating. You will want to keep the achievements separate, or you risk robbing your resume of its own originality. *Save your top achievement(s) for your cover letter.*

Tell what not how

Spare your reader lengthy explanations of *how* you accomplished what you did. *How* you accomplished what you did is of no real interest *now* to your reader. *What* you did is what is of real interest. You make your cover letter shorter, and it can be read in half the time.

There is one notable exception to tell-what-not-how. If how you did it shows you as unique, ingenious, or shrewd and resourceful, then by all means get credit for it in your cover letter without waiting to be asked about it in the interview.

In the John Rubenstein letter (Sales, page 150), the writer relates what could be a lengthy anecdote in a mere eight lines. He leaves out all the details of what it takes to go from zero to a 50% share of Wal-mart's hosiery sales, except for two:

1. "I arranged with the mill to keep case stock on hand for faster deliveries to Wal-mart."

2. "I created a 10-pack promotion that sold 100,000 dozen."

The 10-pack did not just tumble down from the clouds fully packaged and labeled. And he may have had to contact several people at the mill and write a few memos to secure the faster deliveries. But all those details are omitted, lest the reader grow bored reading them.

Okay to leave out date, place and employer's name

In a cover letter, unlike a resume, custom does not require you to give the dates accomplishments were performed, or the place. Not even the name of the employer for whom they were performed needs to be mentioned. Nor are you required to present your achievements in the chronological order they were performed.

What to do if you're part of a team

Maybe you're thinking to yourself, "My job was different. . . . I worked as part of a team. . . . I can't separate my results from that of the others." The rule here is simple enough. Show what the *group* did. Measure your own input against other members of the team. Mention any profit-aiding or time-saving suggestions of yours the team adopted. The truth is the company is the team, and each employee in it, from file clerk to president, is a team member. You can make a contribution to company profits merely by doing your job better than anyone has done it before you.

I was part of a three-person management team that took over an unprofitable supermarket doing $100,000 a week. We slashed pilferage to rock bottom and the store got profitable.

Measure/quantify your accomplishments

This I can certify to. Businesspeople like accomplishments put to them in numbers, percentages, dollar signs, before-and-after comparisons. Precise, factual measurements of your achievements create indelible mental images of your capabilities.

Difference between accomplishments and benefits

Benefits go one step further than accomplishments. A benefit is the *outcome* of what you accomplish. A benefit focuses on what the accomplishment *does for the employer*. The question—always—is not what will your accomplishment do? But what will it do for *me*?

Everything you say in your cover letter must be said in a way that always answers this important question. First announce the accomplishment; then show how the employer benefits.

In the following two examples, the accomplishment is shown first in the regular typeface, then the benefit deriving from that accomplishment is shown in italics:

1. While Head Electromechanical Engineer, I introduced copper alloy fittings—*securing new sales of high-temperature and high-load applications not previously possible*.

2. For a manufacturer of women's blouses, I developed from scratch a new line of blouses for department stores *that raised company sales 40%—in one year*.

In the first example, improving the product is *not* an accomplishment of itself. Without the improved product leading to increased sales "not previously possible," the accomplishment standing alone might have resulted in increased manufacturing costs only.

Ditto for the second example. Developing a new line of blouses for department stores of itself is not such a great feat. Anyone who can sew can develop a line of blouses for department stores. The trick is in developing a line that is bought with both hands by department store buyers, and lifts sales 40% in a brief time period. That 40% sales gain is the *benefit* to the employer of this accomplishment. Had the new line been unwanted by department store buyers, it would be a costly embarrassment, not an accomplishment.

As a space saver, many cover letters jump straight to the benefit and skip the accomplishment, e.g., "Increased sales 40% in a brief period." The new blouse line that started the sales surge is unmentioned. As I said earlier, there is certainly no need to belabor the reader with *how* an accomplishment was achieved, only *what*. In describing your accomplishments, however, the *how* part (accomplishment) is so closely linked to the *what* (benefit), you will profit by describing both.

For one thing, you add instant credibility. "Increased sales 40% in a brief period," may be a clever writer's way of dramatizing a one-time happening—maybe the 40% gain was pure luck. Whereas, by adding the words, "For a manufacturer of women's blouses, I developed from scratch a new line of blouses for department stores," you show the source of the benefit. Moreover, with the phrase "developed from scratch," you imply the benefit is repeatable for anyone who hires you. Finally, it takes so very few extra words to include both the accomplishment and the benefit that sprang from it—you gain very much for very little.

An unbroken presentation of strong benefits justifies and rewards the reader for continuing to read. You will see examples in this book of two-page letters, based on that premise. To know what constitutes a benefit to the employers you wish to reach, you want to know—or acquire—an understanding of what employers in that industry are doing, their special needs, their headaches and how the benefit you offer will affect their daily activities.

By presenting a flow of benefits you know your target employer really wants, you are virtually assured your cover letter will be read carefully. Realize, however, *telling* the employer your work is beneficial is in no way parallel to *convincing* the reader with concrete, factual examples.

Let me hasten to add here that there are exceptions. You cite benefits when they are known or can be determined and measured. I realize this is not always possible. For example, I have helped over two dozen fashion designers with their cover letters. Several designers told me they were not told the sales figures, reorders, etc., for their lines by their bosses, the apparel manufacturers. It seems the manufacturers prefer not to inform designers of sales results, fearing requests for raises from designers who sense they are hot. Still, there are ways for a designer to look good in a cover letter (see Fashion Designer, page 122).

Accomplishments checklist

What accomplishments interest employers? They are interested in anything that will improve the operation of the business and lead to increased profits.

Employers look for your ability to do certain critical things well. Edwin L. Artzt, former chairperson of the Procter & Gamble Co., defined what he looked for in his executives in a speech titled "The What-Counts Factors," given at the Wharton Graduate School of Business, University of Pennsylvania, March 2, 1988:

1. Consistently handling a large volume of work well.

2. Having a healthy dissatisfaction with the status quo.

3. Managing and developing people (taking an active role in training and motivating others to get results).

4. Analyzing facts quickly and arriving at sound conclusions and practical plans of action.

5. Communicating clearly, concisely and persuasively, orally and in writing.

6. Ability to win against someone or some force trying to beat you.

Think back over things you've done at places you've worked. Things that made your job, your department, maybe the whole company run smoother and more profitably. It's astounding what accomplishments a careful search of your work record can bring to the surface.

Here's a checklist I've made to help trigger your recall:

1. **Saved time** — You did assigned tasks in less time than it took predecessors (others) to make sales calls, typing, counting, deliveries, payroll, assignments, etc.

2. **Computers** — You bought/leased/installed a new system? Enhanced existing system? Got bugs out of existing system?

3. **Wrote reports** — You wrote clearer, briefer reports? Got higher readership? Gave more details? Fewer? Discontinued obsolete reports? Provided new ones?

4. **Absenteeism** — You were always present and on time? Left sick days unused? Always available for overtime? (Virtues in entry-level jobs.)

5. **Cut overhead** — You slashed electric bill? Phone (long-distance calls)? Air express? Stationery? Fuel? Legal? Accounting? Insurance? Cut employee pilferage?

6. **Sales** — You sold more than others? Made more cold calls? More profit per sale? Revived dormant accounts? Opened new territories? Won contests, bonuses, trips, citations?

7. **Customer service** — You cut down customer returns? Handled complaints faster? Revised letters, phone policies? Changed policies? Were praised for your handling of difficult customers?

8. **Safety** — You made workplace safer? Cleaner? Cut incidence of workplace accidents?

9. **People** — You raised morale? Learned everyone's name? Cut staff turnover? Changed work rules? Scheduling? Hired superior staff? Introduced suggestion system to get feedback on needed improvements? Trained staff? Fired staff (shows decisiveness)?

10. **Purchasing** — You bought merchandise/supplies cheaper from same suppliers? Found new low-cost suppliers? Better terms than previously? Faster delivery? Got greater discounts? Improved quality? Improved vendor relationships? Cut inventories? Counted them faster, with fewer staff? Took inventory oftener? Less often? Leased equipment previously bought (or vice versa)?

11. **New products/new lines** — You suggested

a new product idea or line? Improved an existing product or line? Found new customers for established products? Cut/expanded product line? Discontinued a losing line/product?

12. **Record keeping** — You set up new records, logs for more accurate reporting and to keep superiors better informed? Furnished more comprehensive reports? Simplified existing record keeping? Discontinued obsolete logs, reports? Converted manual record keeping to computer?

13. **Productivity** — Automated plant, office, a department? Introduced incentive plans? Improved quality? Cut out bottlenecks? Cut overtime? Slashed paperwork? Improved systems, quality?

14. **Advertising** — You created a successful campaign? Increased readership/response? Got more leads per dollar invested? Introduced new media? Cut ad production costs?

15. **Budgets** — You can draw up a budget? Stick to it? Come in below it?

16. **Banking** — You changed to a better bank? Had monthly fees cut? Got loan for company, previously denied? Arranged lower interest, better terms? Earned money with overnight investments of surplus cash?

17. **Recommended against any of the aforementioned** — You saved organization from making a costly mistake?

The you attitude (you, your, yourself, us, our, we)

There is one topic in which all the employers out there will forever be interested — themselves. In this characteristic of human nature lies the clue to your understanding and applying the force of the you attitude to increase the responses to your cover letters. Peoples' interest — you, me and the rest of us — is first, last and always in *themselves*. When a test panel of university students was given a new fountain pen to test, 96% wrote their own names. In his book, *How to Write A Good Advertisement*, Victor Schwab points out that, in the best 100 headlines ever written, forty-three contain one of

these three words: *you, your, yourself*.

When you utilize these six words — *you, your, yourself, us, our, we* — you transfer to your reader a feeling of involvement and participation. You make the employer's concerns your concerns: Let's not talk about me, but about what I am prepared to do for you. You put yourself in close communion with your prospective employer whose first thought isn't what can you do, but what can you do for *me*? "Why should I hire you?" is a favorite question of employment interviewers.

Take the spotlight off yourself

Reinforce your appeal by allowing your prospective employer to play the leading role in your cover letter. Make your prospective employer's interests, aims, worries and wishes the chief topics of your letter, and you will be discussing the most fascinating topics in the world — to that employer.

At the turn of the 20th century, a newspaper advertising salesperson was attempting to sell an advertising campaign to Charles Schwab, president of the United States Steel Corporation. Advertising was then still in its infancy and few knew much about it at all, much less its powerful powers of persuasion. Schwab told the salesperson, "No one reads advertising," and the ad salesperson said, "I will come back with an ad I guarantee you will read." The salesperson returned and handed Mr. Schwab a full-page newspaper advertisement with the headline "This ad is all about the rise of Charles Schwab."

See through the employer's eyes

If you're after results, translate every achievement of yours into terms of its pertinence and benefit to the employer you are writing to. Let me give you some examples of the you attitude in action from cover letters in this book:

I want to help you to run your office in such a way as will make the whole company respect and admire its efficiency.

Some of the things you said in your ad make me feel you are searching for a controller with my experience. My background matches all of your ad's requirements. I write reports that get your attention. I install information systems that permit you to access every bit of information critical to the success of your business. Systems I have designed let you plan ahead and even project the future on a day-to-day basis.

I have a few ideas I'd like to talk to you about, and then you decide if I might be useful to your future.

Because you are involved in sourcing, you know improperly prepared documents are one of the biggest sources of headaches and delays.

I have that winning spirit with regard to customer service, and I feel I can greatly and quickly put it to use to benefit your own organization.

Often, your promise to protect the prospective employer from an undesirable condition or consequence also expresses a you attitude:

If a customer leaves your premises dissatisfied, that customer will tell an average of six other people, and never fail to recall the affront whenever your name is mentioned in conversation.

Want to see some examples of the you attitude at work in the advertising we read? As I already noted, forty-three of the most effective headlines ever written use the words *you, your, yourself*. The you attitude dominates the thinking of every advertising copywriter (of whom, I had the honor to be one). *Because it pays off in up to double the readership, and readers stay with you twice as long.* Here are two typical examples from advertising:

"If you'd like to eat better, try some of these. They're your ticket to more nutritious meals. And they'll even make your food bills easier to swallow. Best of all, food stamps are free. So you go ahead and dig in."

—From a subway poster urging eligible people to apply for food stamps

"Perhaps you've got your heart set on sailing the high seas. With a cool $10 million to your name, you can don a captain's hat on your very own yacht. One of the Ten Personal Super Prize Numbers assigned to you in this bulletin could turn your dreams into real lifetime adventures. Remember, one entry makes you eligible for all the prizes in this bulletin, so be sure you enter by January 24."

—Advertisement for Publisher's Clearing House

We, our and us are equally effective

Blend the words *we*, *our* and *us* into your sentences and they are equally as bonding as *you, your* or *yourself*:

Both of *us* have the same vision for General Electric's future, so let *us* work together to accomplish *our* vision.

Have you ever asked yourself, "How do external users—shareholders for instance—feel about the financial figures *we* accountants provide?"

Summary

Certainly there is plenty of evidence employers hire emotionally as well as logically. The cover letter writer who is after results, therefore, provides what the employer will consider sound reasons (accomplishments) to vindicate the employer's emotional hiring decision.

No amount of self-praise can sell you as effectively as a listing of *specific, measured accomplishments*. Your inability to specify and quantify accomplishments, and the benefits that flow from them to the employer, equals lower response.

Remember the *you* attitude. Don't think so much about what *you* want to write as about what your prospective employer prefers to read, and you will be one enticing step nearer to getting the responses you are looking for.

CHAPTER 7

Devices — Mechanical and Literary

It is a fact that eye-catching layout and literary devices contribute greatly to the attention-getting power of our cover letters.

The more you can keep the employer reading by varying the monotony of conventional sentence and paragraph formats, the better your chances are of creating interest in a personal interview. And the more interesting your letter appears, the longer you will retain your hold.

Visual aids pay a bonus in extra readership

Devices are used to help you break up long sentences and solid paragraphs of type that cause readers to flip the page. You have seen people browsing through books in libraries and book stores. What are they browsing for? Readability. Will the book be an easy read or tediously slow going? The reader's pleasure from reading your letter fades in exact ratio to the amount of work the reader feels it will take.

Readability, or *easy reading*, therefore, is vital because employers like their cover letter information in condensed form and simple language. Your readers will appreciate any devices you provide that help them to grasp the message quickly.

Mechanical devices

Mechanical devices include highlighting, special uses of punctuation, the use of bullets and asterisks, etc.

Highlighting

Highlight with a yellow, see-through, highlighter pen, usually one sentence, or even one paragraph. The uncommonly bright contrast of the yellow ink against the white page captures a reader's attention instantly. However, use highlighting with restraint. No more than one or two highlighted words, phrases or sentences to a letter, or you rob the device of its power of attraction.

The virgule (diagonal, slash mark, /)

In writing you use punctuation marks to make your meaning clear and to send signals to your reader. Periods are *stop* signs. Semicolons and commas are *pause* signs—they signal your reader to merely slow down without really stopping.

I often replace the comma and semicolon with a diagonal or slash mark (/) with a space before and after. I feel it is less interruptive to reading than the comma, and certainly less than the semicolon. I think it allows the reader little pauses for breath, shows where the next idea starts, and carries the reader along effortlessly as though on an escalator.

I never use slash marks in formal writing, but it fits right into the cover letter's format, where almost anything goes. Employers look favorably on symbols of originality. For example:

My office responsibilities include hiring and training of clerical staff / preparation of payroll / scheduling of vacations / buying office supplies and services.

What Aristotle said of drama is true of written

fiction: The work must contain plot / character / theme / story / spectacle.

I believe the slash mark provides somewhat greater clarity than a comma in complex listings:
Software: NATURAL 2.16 and 1.2, ADABAS 4.8, structured COBOL, JCL

Or:
Software: NATURAL 2.16 and 1.2 / ADABAS 4.8 / structured COBOL / JCL

The dash (--)

We use the dash to help us gain attention and to list details. The formal dash is formed by hitting the hyphen key twice, and without spacing preceding or following the two hyphens (--).

I was promoted from laborer to assistant foreman--after only three months--over three other workers who had been there longer.

However, I have this theory about using the double hyphen (--), that visually it acts to *join* two parts of a sentence, rather than set one part off for emphasis. I prefer using a *single* hyphen effect (–) because I feel it *separates* and spotlights the word or phrase you wish set off by dashes. In the previous example, this is how it would look with my single dash mark:

I was promoted from laborer to assistant foreman – after only three months – over three other workers who had been there longer.

Incidentally, *The New York Times* has adapted for its use a dash just like this one, except their hyphen is 50% longer than the traditional keyboard hyphen. If *The New York Times* now licenses the practice, you can proceed with impunity to use a single hyphen as a dash mark, with spaces on either side.

Dashes are helpful also in tabulations. They lead the reader from one point to another, as in this example:

I supervise one manager, and seven technical

and clerical staff:
– cross train personnel to cover for illness and vacation.
– maintain ongoing career development program for staff.
– improved employee satisfaction awareness level from 78% to 86%.
– learned sign language to better relate to two deaf staff members.
– at least 12 employees under my direct supervision have won "Employee of the Month" awards.

Imagine what an imposing, gray block of text the above description would look like if it were expressed in one paragraph, using conventional sentences.

We can also use a dash before the last word(s) in a sentence to add more power to the thought those words express, as in this example:

I understand the role the customer service representative must play in holding on to customers – after they are sold.

Finally, use a dash before the author's name when you attribute a quotation:

"Don't sell the steak, sell the sizzle."
—Elmer Wheeler, *Tested Sentences That Sell*

Italic / Underline

Just as we used the dash to help us draw attention to a word or phrase, we can also use the underline or the *italic* for the same purpose. When you use the underline or italic, you signal to the reader, "I am raising my voice here for emphasis."

"When do you use which?" you may be wondering. It really doesn't matter. What's important is to use the underline or italic with *restraint*. Save them for use on words and phrases that truly merit it. You may find yourself stressing things the importance of which the reader can discover unaided.

Bullet (●)

Bullets can be used to separate points that, used in sequence in a sentence, would make the sentence long and unwieldy, and would rob each other of impact. Example:

My office responsibilities include hiring and training of clerical staff, preparation of payroll, scheduling of vacations, buying office supplies and services and maintaining office equipment.

Better:

My office responsibilities include the following:
● Hire and train clerical staff.
● Prepare payroll.
● Schedule vacations.
● Buy office supplies and services.
● Maintain office equipment.

Note that each bullet listing ends with a period, because each is a sentence. The subject, *I*, is understood, i.e., I hire and train clerical staff. I prepare payroll.

Asterisk (*)

The asterisk's most frequent use is as a reference to a footnote at the bottom of the page. When so used, put the asterisk at the end* of the word or words connected to the reference and at the beginning of the footnote.

The asterisk can also be used in place of bullets to introduce items in a vertical list, for those who use a typewriter and do not have access to a word processor or computer that typesets bullets.

Office closing procedures:
* Turn off lights and copier.
* Turn off air conditioner.
* Lock door in two places.

Ellipses (. . .)

Ellipses, expressed by three periods (. . .), are used to indicate a word or phrase has been omitted from a sentence . . . or to signal the reader to pause a moment before reading further.

Ellipses, you will find, are a great aid to making long sentences seem shorter . . . through frequent pauses . . . and by breaking the pieces of information into little bite-size, readable chunks . . . as in these examples:

You have all the elements needed for success, including talent . . . sharp faculties . . . ability to read people . . . a good head for numbers . . . and you're profit conscious.

Every time I phone or call on a prospective account, I come with an idea . . . a proposal . . . a counterproposal . . . a phenomenal seller to recommend.

I have not shown examples where the ellipse is used to indicate words have been omitted. If you are quoting others, and the matter is so lengthy as to require ellipse marks for omitted portions, then you ought to condense the material or find a shorter quote.

Subheads

Use subheads and you take one desirable step further in devices to make your cover letter *look* like easy reading. Subheads, with their pertinent curiosity appeals, are intended to break up large blocks of text and get your reader deeper into the body of the letter.

Just to show you how important this function can be, the American Newspaper Publishers Association reported that the average newspaper reader reads past the first paragraph in only one of every four articles started.

Questions make very good subheads. Or have your subhead tell a quick, ministory of its own—to slow down the glance-at-a-few-lines-and-run reader. Any subhead promising a strong benefit the reader is known to want never fails to lure the reader into going on.

Literary devices

Literary devices include the P.S., use of repetition, use of quotes, questions, etc.

The P.S.—the best-read part of your cover letter

The great American humorist Mark Twain told the story of an anxious mother who told him about her two sons, away at school, who failed to respond to her many letters. Twain suggested she end her next letter to her sons with the following P.S.: "I am enclosing $5 for each of you to spend as you wish," then omit enclosing the money. Her sons responded by return mail, inquiring about the missing $5.

The P.S. attracts curiosity because, first of all, it is easy reading. It is set off by itself with wide spacing before and after. And it consists of no more than a sentence or two. Second, the reader is curious as to what conclusion or fact the writer felt must not be left out and deserved this special spotlighting.

Your well-expressed P.S. presents a final opportunity to make the employer feel safe, to add one final note of credibility to your candidacy and to help rid the employer of any lingering doubts.

Examples of the P.S. in cover letters abound throughout the book.

Repetition of key words and phrases

Low costs bring low prices, and low prices bring customers.

Still tongues bring interviews, and interviews bring job offers.

I have the talent, I have the knowledge, I have the skills, and I may be reached at (215) 555-5394.

Repetition of chief words and phrases (1) livens your cover letter with a graceful cadence (the rhythmic flow of a sequence of words or musical notes), and (2) drives home your point by presenting it in a cause-and-effect framework, a ministry always with a happy ending.

Direct quotation

Direct quotation (dialogue) is nothing more than repeating *exactly* what people said, in their own words. Quotations liven up your cover letter because you are writing the way people talk. For example:

One Friday afternoon, my boss unexpectedly asked me if I would be available for overtime that weekend, and I told him I would.

You can convert this to a direct quotation:

"Would you be available for overtime this weekend? I could really use you . . ." my boss asked me unexpectedly one Friday afternoon, and I said, "Sure!"

Direct quotation is the most readable form of writing. The comics are one of the best-read sections of any newspaper. Quotations are useful in summing up a situation, or in setting mood to introduce a topic. Or, they can be used to express your own feelings about what you are writing about. The next time you pick up a copy of *Reader's Digest*, *The Wall Street Journal*, *Rolling Stone*, or any other mass-circulation periodical, see if you do not find the major articles consist of one-third or more of direct quotation.

So far we have spoken of using only direct quotations from work-related conversations. You can also use quotes from books, articles, speeches and so forth to invigorate your letters or to make a point:

Socrates said, "To instruct, we must first entertain."

Where do you find quotations that are not already worn threadbare from overuse? There is enough aboveground supply to last everyone now writing cover letters another 40 years. I went to my local book store to find a bibliography for use here. Here is a list of 10 titles I chose from about 30 available on the shelves:

- *Modern Humorous Quotations*, compiled by Fred Metcalf, Penguin Books, 1987
- *The Little Brown Book of Anecdotes*, edited by Clifton Fadiman, Little, Brown & Co., 1967
- *637 Best Things Anybody Ever Said*, Robert

Byren, Fawcett, 1986

- *The Viking Book of Aphorisms: A Personal Selection*, by W.H. Auden and Louis Kronenberger, Penguin Books, 1971
- *Isaac Asimov's Book of Science and Nature Quotations*, Weidenfeld and Nicholson, 1989
- *Barnes & Noble Book of Quotations*, HarperCollins, 1990
- *Simple Truths, A Collection of Wit, Wisdom, Humor and Beauty*, edited by Harry B. Otis, Andrews & McNeel, 1986
- *The Concise Columbia Book of Quotations — Over 6,000 Remarks, Witticisms, Judgments and Observations*, Avon Books, 1991
- *Instant Quotation Director*, Dell, 1990
- *The Pocket Book of Quotations*, Pocket Books, 1986

If you are unsure whether the quotation you are using is broadly known or relatively unknown, then safeguard yourself by using a *disclaimer* (a word or sentence that qualifies another statement):

As you have heard many times, "If you want something done give it to a busy person."

Or, show your agreement with the quotation:
Barnum was right when he said, "A sucker is born every minute."

Parenthetical expressions

Parenthetical expressions (from the Greek *parenthet* — putting in beside) are pieces of relevant but unneeded information enclosed in parentheses within the body of a sentence. They are intended to (1) provide the reader with more information, and (2) by breaking the sentence into separate parts, make it seem shorter and easier to read. Examples:

I placed third in the "Wall Street Sweepstakes" contest (out of over 12,000 who entered).

I started with the company as warehouse manager (the fifth person to fill that position in three years).

Of course, the same parenthetical expressions can be set off with commas. But then you have the physical appearance of one long sentence, rather than two short ones, e.g.:

I started with the company as warehouse manager, the fifth person to fill that position in three years.

No punctuation is required for the parenthetical matter within the parentheses. (If you should choose to enclose a complete sentence within the parentheses, then use a period or some other punctuation mark *within* the parentheses.) If your parenthetical material ends the sentence, then place the period or other punctuation mark *outside* the parentheses (as you see done here).

Ask a question

What other device can we use to involve our reader? Asking a question of your reader is an excellent way of bonding the two of you. You can use a question at the start, in the middle, at the end, anywhere you want to. Just be sure it is a question certain to trigger only one train of thought in the employer's mind. The train of thought you want triggered.

Questions with a question mark at the end, unlike rhetorical questions (where no answer is expected), have two or more possible answers. You must be certain your answer leads the employer to reach the conclusion you want reached. (See Chapter 3, Jump-Start Opening.)

Work-related anecdotes or incidents

You may use an incident, an anecdote, or some other work-related personal experience to appeal to the employer's curiosity or feelings, because most people like to listen to or read stories. Highly entertaining letters are likely to attract twice as many readers because they are so readable.

The formula for using a work-related anecdote or incident in your cover letter is simple. Just furnish a quick, tightly drawn description of a problem or crisis you faced with which your prospective employer is familiar. Then describe the favorable outcome you helped to bring about.

As with listing your accomplishments, tell *what* favorable result you obtained, not *how*. By telling just the *what*, you can reduce your anecdote or incident to a few brief, manageable sentences. Save the *how* for your interviews.

Connectives

Connectives are transitional words, phrases or sentences you put into your cover letter to unify its composition, and to lead your reader smoothly from one thought into the next. Or, you can use them to connect two independent but related sentences. They also serve to intensify the idea you wish to put across. There are dozens of connective words and phrases; here are just a few:

therefore	for instance	finally
for example	to sum up	however
hence	similarly	what's more
moreover	furthermore	nevertheless

I have never been absent or missed a day's work in the past six years. I have never even been late.

Now add a connective like *what's more*, and you intensify the point you are making:

I have never been absent or missed a day's work in the past six years. What's more, I have never even been late.

Other examples of connectives used to intensify:

The snow storm blocked roads and left us short-handed in sales help for the biggest sale of the winter. Nevertheless, we beat last year's results by 18%.

I always exceed my sales quota regardless of business conditions. For instance, during the recession year of 1991, I was still ahead 8%.

Connective sentences can also be useful in a cover letter at the beginning or end of a paragraph, to signal your reader you are finished discussing one subject and want to switch to another:

I have gone miles out of my way to make customers comfortable and win their approval. Customers are the mainspring of everything, I feel. *Which brings me to the point of my letter.*

I am familiar with LANs, operating systems, PCs, IBM and DEC hardware, and I have been using the VAX/VMS Timesharing System. *But that's not nearly all.*

Something else you ought to know about me is I have also worked in a consulting capacity. For example, I analyzed the internal controls of Unilever, conducted a system study of Nestle Co., and prepared a report to management on a Japanese-Sri Lankan joint venture. *The whole point I am trying to make here is*, I perform three needed functions, not just one.

Use short words and sentences

Words and sentences cost you nothing. You can give your prospective employers as many as they choose to read. My suggestion is to use as few as possible and to use simple words of one syllable (words like *and*, *them*, *deal*, *you*, *here*) wherever you can.

I also suggest you use short sentences averaging 15 words in length. If one sentence is 23 words long, another should be only 7.

I further suggest no paragraph of straight text in your cover letter exceed *six* lines in length. Six lines is absolute. That is, you won't have a four-line paragraph followed by an eight-line paragraph, for an average of six lines per paragraph.

Additionally, mix your paragraph lengths. Your opening, of course, will be no more than two or three lines. Try to follow the opening with a second paragraph of no more than four lines. Three is better. Then, in your third paragraph, you can write up to six lines. Avoid following one six-liner with another—aim for four to five lines in your fourth paragraph.

Polysyllables (from the Greek word *polysyllabos*, of many syllables) are words of two syllables or more, e.g., ex-am-ples (three syllables) / ex-per-i-ence (four) / pro-fit (two) / pro-fit-a-ble (four) / pro-fit-a-bil-i-ty (six).

"Put this down as a truth for writing of any kind of copy that seeks to influence behavior — simple short words do the best job," says Frailey in *Handbook of Business Letters*. I could give you several dozen similar quotes.

Ordinarily, repetitive use of one-syllable words in formal writing is as monotonous as hard rain on a tin roof. But they are ideally suited to communications *intended to be brief* — like business letters, reports, speeches, manuals of instruction, etc.

Short, simple words hold the reader's interest longer than long, difficult words. Several formulas have been compounded by writing instructors, particularly Frailey and Flesch, to guide you in your strict use of monosyllables.

The formulas are quite simple. You count *all* words in the text of your cover letter, leaving out proper nouns (names of persons, places or things). We'll call this number A. Next, count only words of one syllable. We'll call this number B. Divide A into B and you have a percentage measurement of your use of one-syllable words in your cover letter. Lincoln's Gettysburg Address is a typical example the word experts use:

268 — total words in Gettysburg Address — A

196 — total words of one syllable — B

Divide A into B, and we get 73%. Lincoln scored a 73.

A score of 70% is a very readable letter. A score of 80% is still more readable, and so forth. Lincoln's personal correspondence is supposed to have scored over 80%.

About 70% is close to the right figure. Letters with that percentage of one-syllable words, or higher, are usually easy to understand, and their chances of success strengthened. Letters with a lower percentage tend to be heavy and ineffective.

Sixty percent or lower and you have a bad language habit. Your letters simply will not do the job if handicapped by an overdose of big words.

You can also use one-word sentences for dramatic emphasis. For example, you have seen people browsing in book stores. What are they browsing for? Readability.

The prospective employer reads quickly, and because the object of your letter is to present your thoughts to the reader in a way that can be easily understood, overlong sentences and complicated words defeat that aim.

Humor

Every employer likes to laugh or smile through reading humorous stories and anecdotes. Freud analyzed relationships between sense of humor and intelligence levels. Employers believe a sense of humor in a job applicant often indicates insight. A humorous quotation, remark or anecdote can add a little more reader involvement to your cover letter that could make it even better.

Naturally there must be a point to your humor, and the point ought to be related to your fitness for the position. Humor has to be handled carefully; it is desirable when it is understated.

Don't set out to write a humorous cover letter. Write a cover letter with humor. No prospective employer must be allowed to feel that we have not taken the job opening seriously. Here are two examples taken from letters used as examples in this book:

When I worked for the New Jersey Vocational Institute, New Jersey state inspectors visited our school one day — but not to get educated. They gave us 72 hours to correct deficiencies or they would close the school. I was assigned to handle the correction.

I tell my friends anthropology is a religious hobby. They ask, "What do you do to practice?" and I tell them, "I ride the subways every day."

Devices to avoid

The following devices are generally best avoided.

Multiple question or exclamation marks for emphasis

Is this not a great accomplishment???

Don't hire anyone until you've read this resume!!!

In each of the previous examples, the writer hopes to triple the importance of what is said by piling on more punctuation marks. But the reader may be put off by your attempt to pump up the significance of a sentence by mechanical means, to make it seem more profound than it is. Readers will attach importance to your statements proportionate to what *they* feel they deserve.

Use of all capital letters

WORDS PRINTED IN ALL CAPITALS ARE HARDER FOR THE EYE TO READ, AND TEND TO SLOW THE READER DOWN. Avoid use of words in all capitals except in headings such as EDUCATION, EMPLOYMENT, SKILLS, etc., which the eye picks up in a single glance.

If you wish certain words to stand out, print them in bold type, or use another of the devices mentioned earlier.

Use of curiosity gimmicks

A gimmick in a cover letter is any tricky device used for its own sake to draw a reader's attention, most often by arousing the reader's curiosity. You can draw a lot of attention with gimmicks—*without* directing any of it toward you and your story.

Curiosity gimmicks rarely pay off. That's because it's so hard to find a gimmick that links you to a benefit the employer really wants.

You can draw a lot of attention with spectacular gimmicks that arouse the prospective employer's curiosity. Except they must draw a lot of attention to yourself and your superiorities. Curiosity gimmicks pay off for you *only* when you tie them straight to the benefit the employer really wants. Physically irrelevant devices detract from the interest and readability of your letter if there is not an immediate and direct link between the gimmick and an employer benefit.

$50,000 Reward to Whoever Hires Me. The April 17, 1992, issue of *National Business Employment Weekly*, tells of an unemployed marketing executive who ran display ads with a headline offering companies a $50,000 reward for hiring him. The ad reads, "This is what you'd have to pay a headhunter to find an executive with my background, track record, and reputation. Listen to my 3-minute recorded history and you decide if we should talk."

That trick, alas, annoyed virtuous employers more than it intrigued them. The executive said he spent about $1,400 on the scheme, got about a half-dozen leads, but no job offer. "I've had a lot of fun," said the jobhunter, "but it hasn't brought home the bacon."

A Spoonful of Sugar. Carl Boll, in *Executive Jobs Unlimited*, says, "Don't waste your time on gimmicks." He tells of a jobhunter who sent out 100 letters to presidents of companies, each containing a spoonful of sugar packaged in cellophane, hoping to sweeten the reception of the letter. The letter said his wife believed he was slightly crazy, but he hoped the gift would get him a 5-minute interview.

If you have to turn to gimmicks to get attention, you are likely to be doing other things improperly also.

Summary

Mechanical and literary devices add liveliness and human interest to cover letters and make them look highly readable to prospective employers. Cover letters that seem to require little effort on the reader's part attract twice as many readers.

CHAPTER 8

Nonsexist Language

You should be aware that half the readers of your cover letter may be women, often in decision-making positions. Women who open letters written in sexist language may not be in much of a hiring mood at the end. We need to make a special effort, therefore, to make our cover letters gender neutral to avoid unintentionally offending innocent readers.

Your incapacity to deal with women executives as equals may deprive your company of business it might otherwise have gotten. Here are some elementary guidelines you will want to put to use in a cover letter you may be writing right now.

Avoid use of words that are not gender neutral

A rule of thumb that will serve you well is to analyze any word in your cover letter with *man* in it — either when used as a prefix, e.g., *manpower, manhours*, or as a suffix, e.g., *foreman, chairman*.

Sexist	Better
salesman	salesperson, sales representative
foreman	supervisor, director, manager
manpower	staff, crew
policeman	police officer
fireman	firefighter
meter maid	meter reader
postman	postal carrier, mail carrier
motorman	driver
paymaster	pay supervisor, cashier
night watchman	night sentry
self-made man	self-made person
anchorman	anchor
organization man	team player
union man	union member
businessman	businessperson, executive, manager
manhandle	mishandle
chairman	chairperson, chair
workman's compensation	worker's compensation
spokesman	spokesperson, speaker
waiter/waitress	server

Beware of wrong assumptions from gender-neutral names

I'm sure you've seen one: a classified or display employment ad that tells you to address your reply to someone named Pat, Chris, Terry, Marty, or some other name that leaves you baffled whether to use Mr. or Ms. as a salutation.

I always took it as a challenge. I reasoned the employer was trying to test me to see how I would respond.

I would simply do the commonsense thing and type the inside address the same as I would any other cover letter:

ATTN: Terry
Box 215
Grand Central Station P.O.
New York, NY 10022

Dear office (sales, purchasing, human
  resources) manager:

It is important to remember here that it is highly
unlikely (except at entry levels, and in some support positions) that Pat, Chris, Terry or Marty will
be the person interviewing you.

More likely, they are merely intermediaries.
Perhaps it is a large office. By using someone's
name on the outer envelope, responses to the ad
can be directed to the proper person to be re-
viewed.

Avoid *Gentlemen:* as a salutation

I am astonished at how many cover letters I see
that still bear the sexist word *Gentlemen* as a salutation. I can't offer you exact statistics, but I'm pretty
sure some women hiring executives wouldn't
touch a letter with that salutation with a ten-foot
pole. This book gives you a half-dozen safe, tested,
gender-neutral ways to begin.

Avoid, also, *Dear Sir/Madame.* As a salutation, it
is colorless, impersonal and musty from age. Use
only the courtesy titles *Mr.* or *Ms.* for all business
correspondence (unless you know a woman prefers
to be addressed as *Mrs.*).

Gender-specific pronouns:
The big obstacle

Let's now tackle the biggest hurdle of them all in
your race to switch to nonsexist language: generic
male pronouns, *he, his* and *him.*

One obstacle for most writers is the old rule
about a singular noun requiring a singular pronoun:

When a *supplier* (singular noun) delivers
  merchandise, *he* (singular pronoun) expects
  to be paid.

Often the easiest choice is to convert to the plural (pluralize):

When suppliers deliver merchandise, they
  expect to be paid.

Because we don't use the gender-neutral singular pronoun *it* to refer to people, we are forced to
consider mixing singular nouns with plural pronouns. A number of authorities I have researched—college professors and the style books
of newspapers and wire services—*all agree* it is now
okay to use a plural pronoun even when the ante-
cedent is singular:

When a *supplier* (singular noun) delivers
  merchandise, *they* (plural pronoun) expect to
  be paid.
When a student fails, they are entitled to an
  explanation.
When a customer enters your store, they are
  looking for something.

This construction may sound a bit awkward
when you first start to use it, but you know that the
future is on your side. This practice of changing
from the singular to the plural in sexist pronoun
dilemmas, is beginning to become quite common-
place, because it avoids gender entirely.

Another way to avoid using sexist language is to
substitute the second person *you:*

When you deliver merchandise, you expect to
  be paid.

Another option that may fit your needs is to
switch to the word *one:*

When one delivers merchandise, one expects to
  be paid.

Or, use *we:*

When we deliver merchandise, we expect to be
  paid.

Or, simply recast the sentence:

When merchandise is delivered, payment is
  expected.

I could provide you with many more examples,
but I think you get the point. Women should re-

ceive the same consideration as men in all your writing. Your treatment of the sexes in your cover letters — indeed, in all your writing — should be free of sexist terms, stereotypes and other patronizing references.

Realize you don't have to be sexist yourself to slip into sexist writing. You may simply have sunk into the groove of habit. You continue, innocently and with the purest of motives, to use language and terms that for a long time were quite acceptable, but are now offensive to many of your readers.

Helpful reference books

There are many books that deal with gender in writing (and a surprising number of books on writing that do not). One is the *U.P.I. Stylebook* (Third Edition, 1992). *The McGraw Hill Style Manual* (edited by Marie M. Longyear, 1989) has a comprehensive discussion complete with a list of helpful guidelines that runs to six pages.

If you have time for but one, comprehensive book on this subject, I recommend a 90-page book, *The Elements of Nonsexist Usage*, by Val Dumond (Prentice Hall, 1990). Dumond gives you sound business reasons for avoiding sexist language and shows you ways to do it. One of the best features of this book is the 14 pages of alternative terms. This list includes hundreds of sexist terms all of us use every day — from *adman* to *watchman*. (I mentioned several examples earlier.) Each sexist term has an alternative gender-neutral term (often two or three).

Summary

It will probably be some time to come before a *chairman* of the board of Exxon, IBM or General Electric is referred to readily as the *chair* or *chairperson*, but we have to start somewhere. Why not catch on now to the nation's spiraling tilt toward the use of gender-neutral terms and titles?

Be observant of nonsexist language in your cover letter. Sexist words and terms can easily be sanitized into nonsexist language, and you are guaranteed to have offended no one. Many alternative words and phrases are available.

This book is written entirely in nonsexist language.

CHAPTER 9

"Please Enclose Salary Requirements..."

A favorite ruse perpetrated on unwary job-hunters by Unequal Opportunity Employers (UOE).

Why unequal?

The next time you read a classified employment ad requesting you to disclose your salary history (for the convenience of this chapter, the S Request), and at the bottom it reads "We are an equal opportunity employer (EOE)" — don't you believe it. By asking in advance for your salary history, these employers strip you of your bargaining power, then invite you in to use it.

"If homes were sold the way jobs are negotiated, we'd want to know what you paid for your house before we made you an offer," is a statement attributed to an insurance company personnel manager by Steve Kravette in *Get a Job in 60 Seconds* (Para Research, Inc., 1982).

No question is asked of me more often and with more fear than, "Should I include my salary in my cover letter?" Executives down to support staff ask it. It is asked ten times as often as any other question I can think of. Even those who ask no other questions ask that one. It's apparent they sense that a wrong answer could make their job chances fly away, even though they were right for the job and wanted it badly.

New survey settles question once and for all

To settle this question — "Should I enclose my salary?" — once and for all, three Vassar College grad-uates and I interviewed by phone 200 companies and not-for-profit organizations who ran display employment ads in *The New York Times*, and the *National Business Employment Weekly*, asking for salary information.

We also interviewed (by mail) 100 executives who have responded to ads asking for salary and *not* given it . . . to give you factual accounts and verbatim comments from the applicants' side. Finally, I wrote to 50 executive recruiters. The interviews took six months to complete and were conducted between January and June, 1992.

1. Survey of 200 employers making the S Request in ads

Employers add the S Request into only 20% of ads. We researched issues of *The New York Times* and the *National Business Employment Weekly* display employment ads that appeared in the months January to May, 1992. We counted a total of 1,352 display employment ads for all sorts of positions — support level, middle management, upper management. Of the 1,352 total ads, 272 asked applicants to include salary information, which amounts to 20%. Of these 272 who asked for salary information, we interviewed 200.

Ninety-four percent of the 200 employers said they consider all responses. Of the 200 organizations we talked to, 187, or 94%, told us they consider every cover letter received.

Only four ads out of the 200 we looked into threatened *not* to consider you if you did not respond to the S Request. So, did they? Of the four who threatened not to, in phone interviews, it turned out two of them were bluffing. One who was, a giant food manufacturer, conceded they considered *all* responses. Here's what their ad said: **"RESUMES WITHOUT SALARY HISTORY WILL NOT BE CONSIDERED."** (Bold type and all caps in original.)

In another of these four "no" ads, the employer actually hedged with a cleverly worded statement: "All responses with current compensation will be acknowledged." Left unsaid is the fact that letters that *do not* mention current compensation will also be looked at.

2. Survey of 100 executives who answered ads with the S Request

This finding that employers will consider *all* applications is further borne out by a mail survey we conducted among 200 members of 14 branches of the 40+ Clubs of America. This is a not-for-profit organization dedicated to assisting executives over age 40 in finding new positions. Over 100 responded to our questionnaire.

Here's what they said:

Q. Have you ever responded to an employment ad asking you to "include salary history with resume," and *not* included salary?
90% Yes   10% No

Q. If yes, did an advertiser ever respond?
74% Yes   26% No

Q. Have you ever included your salary and *not* gotten a response from the employer?
76% Yes   24% No

This 40+ Club survey determined that 75% of 100 executives who flaunted the S Request still got responses. With the remaining 25% who did not get responses, one wonders if it was the cover letter and resume rather than nonmention of salary that got yawns from prospective employers.

Here are a few comments from the 40+ Club members:

"I know of at least one job I lost out on because I told the employer my last salary too early in the process. He felt it was too little (at $48K), making me unworthy of consideration for his $75K job."

"This is a discriminatory practice."

"If my qualifications match their needs, salary history is not important."

"It is worth the gamble; I don't like giving salary history before I know more about the job."

"My policy is simple: Don't."

"Company responded, but no interview resulted because I gave salary history on the phone. I will not be furnishing salary information in the future."

"This is merely another, far more subtle, act of employer unfair hiring practices."

I ought to mention here the 40+ Club philosophy as to furnishing salary in advance of an interview. The president of the 40+ Club of Puget Sound Association told me:

We teach members to avoid, if at all possible, any discussion of a salary figure until after the job has been offered. We feel that items such as vacation, parking, options, etc., could very well be part of the package and therefore negotiable. The word "negotiable" when referring to salary desired is the best way to go.

You can expect a phone call. Here's something else that will reassure you as to the wisdom of never disclosing your salary in your cover letter.

About half of the 40+ Club executives who said they had not listed salary history reported getting a phone call from the prospective employer to discuss salary.

Calling hot prospects at home to ask about salary

is a favorite middle ground employers take when they like the look of you on paper so much they begin to wonder if they can afford you. Employers will then pick up the phone and call you at home in the evening or on a weekend and, after exchanging a few pleasantries, get to the point: How much do you cost? Are your money requirements within their range? If they are not, the employer has expended just a fraction of the time it would take to interview you in person.

If you should find yourself tongue-tied when you're asked for your salary in a phone interview, you'll find six appropriate responses further on in this chapter. This willingness to call you at home reveals how highly the employer regards you as a contender for the position. Here are typical comments from our survey of 200 employers:

> "If we are interested, we will call to find out what a person wants."
> —Human Resources Dept., large conglomerate

> "We prefer that it [salary] be enclosed, but if they have the perfect requirements, we'll call them to discuss salary requirements."
> —Human Resource Dept., major computer software maker

> "If it is requested, we appreciate it. It's a hindrance if they don't include it, but we still will call them if they are right for the job."
> —Human Resources Dept., major Japanese electronics manufacturer

From your prospective employer's phone call, you now know you are wanted. You have become a contender. You already have one foot in the door. Hold out for a face-to-face interview. Why throw your hand in just when you start to be in a strong position.

3. Survey of 50 executive recruiters

We also surveyed 50 executive recruiters. I ought to mention at the start that recruiters (and employment agencies), like the employers for whom they work, are also interested in rapidly screening out applicants whom they deem unfit for the position.

Nevertheless, about half the recruiters who responded said they generally agreed with an applicant's not sending salary information in a cover letter. Here's one of the questions they were asked:

Q. What would *you* do if you answered an employment ad that asked you to enclose your salary history?

A. Yes—provide salary if requested:

> "In some cases I would."
> —New York City recruiter

> "Should definitely comply with employer request; use general ranges, possibly salary expectations."
> —California recruiter

> "Would advise to disclose it if the request was made."
> —Florida recruiter

> "I'd give current salary."
> —New York City recruiter

A. Yes . . . and . . . No:

> "Good question! But you have to say something. This question has to be answered but just don't be too specific until you have to be."
> —New York City recruiter

> "Either leave it out, or give a salary range."
> —New York City recruiter

> "I would not send a salary history. I might indicate minimum salary requirements."
> —California recruiter

A. No—don't provide it:

> "Never put in salary. Sell yourself first, and discuss salary later. The first one who

mentions salary loses.''
    —New Mexico recruiter

''I suggest one puts 'open,' or 'will be happy to discuss in interview.' ''
    —Texas recruiter

''No.''
    —New Jersey recruiter

''Do not disclose salary; however, be sure resume and cover letter will prompt employer to call and inquire.''
    —California researcher

Here's a question on which the recruiters were in unanimous agreement:

Q. Do you agree that employers spend so much money and time writing and placing an employment ad they will skim *every* response—regardless of whether salary history is given?
100% Yes   0% No

Typical comments include:

''Yes, one can always call and get salary info; background is more important.''
    —New York City recruiter

''Yes, they feel they have an investment and want to get their money's worth.''
    —Pennsylvania recruiter

''Yes, skim is the right word. If the candidate has the appropriate experience, the resume gets a closer look.''
    —California recruiter

''Yes. Resumes that do not fit a specific advertised position now, may be considered for another area.''
    —Indiana recruiter

The real lesson of the surveys

The fear of being turned away simply because you did not provide salary when asked is a ground-less fear. It is a myth, a fiction. You are far more likely to be disqualified, or to leave money on the table when you are hired, if you do provide your salary history. It is strictly an employers' device for screening people out and bargaining with those left—don't fall for it. Don't disclose salary prematurely even if they put you to the torch.

Reasons organizations ask for salary history

Here are some other insights into employers' feelings we got from our phone interviews.

We asked employers what their reasons are for peering into your salary history. In our survey of 200 employers, 81% responded that it was ''to screen people out.'' Typical comments were:

''To weed out having to interview so many people, particularly those who want too much money.''
    —Textile processor

''To save the applicant time. If he wants more than we can pay, then we won't waste his time.''
    —Service company

''So we can tell what the person is making and then be able to negotiate.''
    —Auto parts supplier to major car makers

''When two people apply for the same position, one might be worth twice as much as the other. It's a way to get a handle on them.''
    —Research organization

''To avoid being inundated with responses.''
    —Truck manufacturer

''To see if someone is on target. It's not to beat them. We pay what we pay regardless of what they want. If they ask for 22K, and the position pays 24K, we pay them 24K.''
    —International commodities firm

"To know if there is any chance the two parties can meet."
—Manufacturer

"To disqualify those who want too much money."
—Major hotel chain

"We set the salary range beforehand and use the ad as a tool to screen out people."
—Financial institution

There are other reasons why employers are curious about salaries of prospective employees. Some employers observe your salary progress to see if you are the type whose only reason for changing jobs is money. It suggests that you may use them as another stepping-stone: "If I see salary requirements, I think the applicant is interested only in money," said one human resources director, who unexplainedly asked for salary requirements in the company's own employment ad.

I ought to mention here another general principle that will profit you: *Avoid giving money as your only reason for changing jobs.*

Employers also seek to gain knowledge of what similar positions pay at other organizations: A large money center bank's human resources chief expressed it this way: "We like to get a feel and compare our salary ranges with others out there."

Why Unequal Opportunity Employer (UOE)?

Salary is and ought to be based on two components: (1) what a job is worth, and (2) the availability of qualified applicants.

Salary cannot fairly be set by you until you have had a chance to determine what the job is worth. Talk always in terms of what a job is worth, not in terms of what you *want*, and never in terms of what you *need*—you don't wish to appear like a pauper at the church door.

Once the job has been described to you in an interview, and only then, can you sensibly decide what a job carrying those responsibilities and the goals the employer wants achieved ought to pay. By quoting a low salary in your cover letter, lower than the employer had expected to pay, you may miss a good chance to have made more. Salaries for a particular position may vary greatly even among companies in the same industry.

This whole business of disclosing salary prematurely in your cover letter is dangerous because it distracts the employer and robs the employer of objectivity. *You no longer are in total control of the employer's first impression of you.* You are now being costed out mentally, and if your salary doesn't fall within the employer's range, your letter is tossed away as though it might pollute the office.

Employers may feel your current salary is excessive for the experience you offer, contrasted with others in the same mail. Being human, they tend to follow the all-too-human tendency to appraise a job applicant in terms of that applicant's highest salary. For example: If you mention $40,000 salary, and the prospective employer has a range up to $55,000 in mind, the employer may feel that $45,000 is a fit starting point to bargain with you.

Some suggested answers

My advice is to leave the subject of salary unmentioned. Ignore the S Request in the ad, and avoid it on the phone. (None of the 100 letters used as examples in this book mentions salary.)

However, if you wish to demonstrate in your cover letter . . . or when you are interviewed on the phone . . . that you are not one to snub your nose at an employer's expressed demand, you might find a version of one of the following explanations useful:

> You may have a salary range in mind. I, too, have no fixed amount in mind. I am open to negotiation.

> With regard to salary, I will leave that open to your own idea of fairness. Salary is negotiable if other important elements are present.

Success in one's career is equated with higher and higher salaries. However, there are people like myself who get their satisfaction from other things besides money.

My salary requirements are flexible. I am sure we can reach an agreement that remains within your guidelines.

May we put off discussion of salary until after we've met, and I have a better understanding of what the job entails? I assure you, it [the S word] will not be a barrier to my employment.

I earn a competitive salary here. But salary isn't the only thing that counts. As far as I'm concerned, I'm more interested in meeting with you and telling you some of the profit-aiding ideas I already have for (company name).

Summary

On the subject of discussing salary before you've had a chance to judge what a job is worth, well, the answer is no, isn't it? Salary *negotiation* (note well that word) is a subject best left to face-to-face discussion.

The employers who will not consider a potential applicant because of the omission of salary information are so few in number—1 in 20—that their absence is unlikely to be a real factor in your job hunt.

Ignoring the S Request will also answer for you the question of whether your failure to hear from an employer was because of salary omission. Now, you'll know, in at least 90% of your mailings, when your cover letter and resume fail to rouse the desired response, it was that the prospective employer liked someone else better than you. In this regard, disregarding the S Request is a good barometer to test the appeal of your cover letter.

Put into your cover letter everything that shows how good you are, and leave everything else out. Salary information—given out in your cover letter or later by phone—is at the top of the list of things that can hurt you and keep you from getting interviews. Still tongues bring interviews, and interviews bring job offers.

CHAPTER 10

Letters for Special Purposes

There are always a few circumstances that crop up for which a letter must be written to fit. I have included a number of letters in this book to cover such special situations.

Relocating to another city

"There is an almost universal tendency to think that others see a problem as we do ourselves. On the contrary, they see the problem from one angle, you from another. Your duty is to see clearly, and understand both points of view."

— William James

The thing to remember when you plan to seek a job in another city is you can't be seen by a prospective employer as fleeing because you can't find a job in your own. You scare employers. Why won't the people in the city you're leaving hire you? Maybe you're hiding something, or running from something. In a word, you are too *available*, in a job market where employers prefer applicants for jobs to be slightly inaccessible.

All the time, employers willingly pay a premium price to capture someone now employed by a competitor, doing the same type of work, and *rising* (through promotions).

Also, there is the question of whether you'll like the new city well enough to stay. One of the most believable (and reassuring) rationales I know for moving to a new city is because one's spouse is being transferred to that city. Or moving to improve the health of a family member. One of the letters used as an example in this category (DeWitt Knapp, page 60) mentions buying a house—a reliable sign of future permanency.

I don't want to make this seem a major problem. I merely wish to point out it is usually harder to find a job in a new city than in one where you are well known—and you ought to be aware of it. The prospective employer ought never be left to wonder, "Do you want to be on *our* payroll, or on *anyone's* payroll?"

Note: Regarding the examples I use to illustrate this section, I could not get in touch with a single person whose letter I intended to use. Their phones were disconnected, and letters to them were returned to me. However, I cannot believe that cover letters as good as some of these are tossed in the wastebasket, so I am including them in this book. Because I have no knowledge of whether these letters got interviews, this fact is noted with each of these letters in the NOTE: at the bottom of each.

Changing careers letters

The advice here is pretty much a reprise of that already given for changing cities. Avoid the impression that you have grown unemployable in your previous career. Wherever possible, furnish the prospective employer a believable reason for wanting to change.

Your resume may not offer much help because it is all about your old career. Consequently your cover letter will have to carry much of the burden of establishing you as a credible contender in your newly chosen career. This is the big difference between changing cities and changing careers.

Acceptable and unacceptable reasons for changing careers

I should point out, by *acceptable*, I mean *emotionally* acceptable. I told you earlier the hiring process is as much emotional as logical.

One of the changing careers letters is by a professional singer seeking administrative work related to the performing arts. Most of us know that professional singers who reach the heights usually fade into twilight as their voices and appearance age. This is an acceptable reason for wanting to change careers.

On the other hand, the fact that there are 1,500 unemployed advertising copywriters in the city of New York is not an acceptable explanation for your leaving New York to seek work elsewhere. Avoid mentioning this fact. An employer wonders why you are not among the 5,000 copywriters still working there? However, if an entire operation is shut down, or is about to be moved to some far-off city unsuitable to you, that is an acceptable reason.

Retirement is usually — not always — not an acceptable reason you would want to mention in your cover letter. It conjures up mental images of someone whose chief work interest lies elsewhere, and strongly suggests an over-the-hill applicant in the mid-fifties or sixties.

The best posture for your letter to assume is to use all of it to show your affinity for the new work. Show any parallel between what you've done and what you will be asked to do. Show a penchant for the new work — something you always felt you would be good at. Wherever you can, show any early indication you like the new work. Go back to your childhood, your school days.

Employers expect specific experience in their fields. What you may lack in specific experience, can to some extent be compensated for by showing a strong aptitude for the work. You will notice in the letter applying for a museum assistant's position (Bernadette McGrath, page 67), the writer (previously a mortgage title researcher) describes her passion for museums in belief-compelling detail.

Letter requesting per diem work

Some of you reading this book may be thinking of seeking less than 40 hours work per week. Please refer to the letter of Walter Wrightsman (Accounting, page 107). Notice the writer offers a skill the employer can use profitably without employing the writer full time.

So, if you're seeking part-time work, stress an area in which you are exceptional, an area where you know your prospective employer can *almost always* be counted on to need assistance. The rule here is sell the employer what the employer wishes to buy, rather than what you have to sell.

Networking letters

About 75% of jobs are gained after first hearing about them from a friend (or friend of a friend) who either has firsthand knowledge of the job, or heard of it from someone else. This is *networking*.

So, it is in your interest to set up a network of friends and other contacts. Realize you never know where a job lead can come from. There is no such thing as a nobody in job hunting.

Networking is just as often carried out by phone as by letter. The letter of Alexander Braun (page 110) is an example of a networking letter to a friend. The letter by Blanche Rosen (page 111) is an example of writing to alumni of your college or university — the old school tie (so named because, in England, graduates of certain select schools wear ties bearing their school's distinctive colors, to be easily recognized by other alumni).

You will find most people, even perfect strangers, quite sympathetic to the plight of those looking for jobs. This is a given, otherwise 75% of jobs would not originate from networking.

The thank-you letter

The letter of thanks for a job interview is the last chance you are likely to get to make a favorable impression on the person who may hire you.

Maybe you're thinking that trying to impress an interviewer after the interview is like feeding soup to the dead. What's the point? Isn't the interviewer's mind already made up about you? Not necessarily.

Two years ago, I surveyed executives for their opinions on hiring issues, including the thank-you letter. The results showed that 59% were still undecided about a hiring decision after an interview, and that more than half (52%) said thank-you letters influenced their decision toward a candidate.

Let me give you three examples of thank-you letters to cover the three possible endings of a job interview.

1. When you are told, "We'll let you know"

Thank you, Mr. Forester:

I realize that interviews rarely end with on-the-spot hiring decisions.

In fact, I wasn't expecting a yes or no answer when we met Thursday morning.

Even so, I appreciate the time you spent with me. I know that only a handful of applicants are invited in for personal interviews, and I'm grateful to have been included among them.

I like the Emerson Electric Co., and I like the job. It's exactly the kind of position in which I know I can excel. Given the chance to prove it, I'm confident that a year from now you'll congratulate yourself for hiring me.

Yours with appreciation,

The point to remember about a thank-you letter is you become a member of a privileged class the moment the prospective employer decides to take a chance on you by inviting you in for a face-to-face interview. There may have been 500 responses, from which yours and a dozen or two others have been selected for follow-up. You have survived the first cut, and an expression of gratitude is in order.

It will do no harm to include a copy of your cover letter and resume. Never take for granted the interviewer remembers you and your story. Fifteen people may have been interviewed after you.

2. When you've been invited back for a second interview

Thank you, Ms. Kennedy . . .

. . . for receiving me so graciously Thursday morning.

I particularly appreciated your efforts to arrange a second interview for me with Mr. Cappell. The information you gave me regarding his department's goals and needs was just what I needed. I feel fully informed and prepared to demonstrate to him how I can make an immediate contribution — thanks to you.

You won't regret having referred me.

With gratitude,

When an interviewer recommends you to someone else for a second interview, that interviewer's own reputation for selecting worthy candidates is now being placed on the line on your behalf. That gesture rates an expression of appreciation.

3. When you have been offered the job — but you asked for time to mull over the offer

Thank you, Mr. Ballard . . . Roger:

I enjoyed our meeting Thursday, and most especially did I enjoy hearing the magic words: "We want you."

Let me assure you right here and now the feeling is mutual. I greatly appreciate your kindness in giving me the time to mull over your job offer and to discuss it with my family.

I realize the ball is now in my court, and I will phone you with my answer within the next 48 hours.

With gratitude,

The point to remember in this version of the thank-you letter is always thank an employer for a job offer. Second, continue to express strong interest in the position. Don't allow your prospective employer to feel you have qualms about the position itself. What about a letter for declining a job offer? Because employers like to know as soon as possible if you do not intend to accept their job offer, this is usually better handled by phone. It permits the employer to contact a second or third choice quickly.

Gratitude is a becoming attitude in your job search. Employers are as human as the rest of us. Interviewing is just a role they play temporarily. They like to be patted on the back for giving someone a leg up in their career, and they're not the only ones. So do secretaries, receptionists, employment agents, recruiters, concerned friends who have given us leads or permitted us to use them as references. All who have done us a good turn in our job hunt deserve, at the very least, an expression of thanks.

A final thought on thank-you letters: If you didn't get a job offer or get invited in for a second interview, many job-advice books counsel you to use your thank-you letter to rehash your virtues or to paper over any bad impression you may have left that might damage you.

In doing so, you run the risk of appearing to have your hand outstretched under the guise of appreciation. Gratitude with strings attached. It could do you more harm than good. If you feel you bungled the interview, better to learn from it and not repeat it in your next interview.

Business-to-business letters

Business-to-business letters are useful for jobhunters who start their own businesses and need a sales letter to get customers. There are two examples in the book of letters soliciting *customers*. One is from a painting contractor (Wade LeMoyne, page 62), and the other is from an expert in employee benefits (Lawrence Gelfand, page 64). Don't be afraid of going to two pages if you need the space to describe the full extent of your services.

The resume is by definition a *summary*, and ditto for the cover letter. Conversely, the business-to-business letter is your complete story. Often, it is accompanied in the same envelope by testimonial letters from satisfied customers, and other promotional enticements such as coupons, price-off offers for first-time customers and so forth.

With slight alterations these letters should serve you well as prototypes on which to model your own sales letters. All such letters ought to end with an action close in which you announce your intention to call the employer. Even more so than in seeking a job, *never leave it to the prospect to call you.*

Summary

Letters for special purposes do not differ in any material way from all the other letters used as examples in this book. The main point to remember is: *Don't dwell on the past.* Start at once to talk about your capacities to perform the new work, and go on talking about them to the end.

CHAPTER 11

The Letters

On the following pages are over 100 actual cover letters in 65 job specialties (see Index) that have brought hundreds of interviews to their writers.

"While individuals may be insoluble puzzles, in the mass they become predictable with mathematical certainty."
—Sherlock Holmes

Each of the 100 cover letters has a brief editorial comment at the bottom noting the reason(s) for the letter's success, and/or giving you deeper, clearer insight into an employer's thinking. No matter how unprofessional your present writing may be, if you follow the guidelines laid down for you at the bottoms of the letters, your own letters will get read. I guarantee it.

A Hollywood screenwriter once said in *Time* magazine, "All the movie westerns ever produced are built around seven basic plots." It's the same

with employers. You will see certain themes repeated over and over again in the letters because they are among a half-dozen basic themes that are endlessly fascinating to every employer. What an employer will think of you, say of you and do for you is directly proportionate to how skillfully you exploit these basic appeals in your cover letter.

In giving their approval for their letters to be used as examples in this book, many of the writers said I needn't bother to change their names and identities. Thank you. Although I have quoted many of their direct comments about the success of their letters, I have followed the policy I have always followed in my articles and substituted new identities for all.

The person has not been found who can squeeze an ice cube in the palm of their hand for 10 minutes. Neither will you find an employer who will not be attracted by the basic appeals expressed in these 100 letters.

Edith N. Cantor, R.N.
34 Woodland Heights Road
Huntington, NY 11710
(516) 555–1781

March 17, 19--

Dear doctor:

There's hardly anything more important in private nursing nowadays than keeping current on illnesses, procedures, devices, treatments, etc.

The more you know about the latest developments, the better you can serve the person you're treating and the doctor employing you. As an example, I read:

RN   *American Journal of Nursing*
Nursing Administration   *Nursing Spectrum*
Nursing '90   All association mail

Additionally, I attend numerous seminars and conferences and take courses to keep current. I attend the EENT convention once a year, as well as the Plastic Surgery Convention, and others. I know all the latest equipment and devices.

I hold a weekly seminar for laryngectomy patients to ease the trauma of voice loss. I enjoy teaching people easy ways to care for themselves. Their smiles console me for everything and repay me for my pains a hundred times.

I am changing my residence to Florida and am seeking a position in private nursing where my comprehensive knowledge of the duties involved, and understanding of what a doctor wants, will be appreciated. I may be reached at (516) 555–1781. Thank you.

Sincerely,

Note: The writer focuses on patient care and the importance of finding new and better ways to do it. The writer moved to Florida, and efforts to reach her to see if she got interviews with her letter have been unsuccessful. Nevertheless, this letter is included as an example of a letter for use in changing cities.

Forester M. Puckett
221 E. Farragaut Street
Atlanta, GA 30324
(404) 555–1614

July 22, 19--

Dear doctor:

Quite honestly, I have no ambition to be a physician, but I am only too happy to be a physician's assistant—and to be the very best.

To that end, I have acquired as much knowledge as I can, and expanded my capabilities to the point where doctors have permitted me to do procedures *they* customarily perform.

I have a degree for a 2-year course in emergency medicine from Ohio State University (in conjunction with Cleveland General Hospital). This is the longest and toughest course of its kind in the country. (In Class No. 9, which is my class, 300 started, 126 finished.) After completing the course, I took the National Emergency Medical Technicians exam. I placed among the top 10% of the thousands who took the test.

In addition to my excellent education, I have diverse experience that cannot be matched by very many other medical assistants. I have worked in two industrial clinics, in an E.M.S. ambulance, and in a cardiologist's office. I love my work, and, with me, the patient in need of healing is the inspiration for everything.

My wife and I are moving to California, and I am seeking a position as doctor's assistant. All of my references are excellent, and I may be reached at (404) 555–1614. Thank you.

Sincerely,

Note: The appeal of this letter is apparent throughout; namely, (1) the writer has been industrious and intelligent enough to plan his education to fit the occupation sought, (2) loves the work, (3) is extremely competent (doctors trust him to perform tasks normally reserved to them). I was unable to contact this writer to see how well this letter did at pulling interviews. But I cannot imagine anyone this qualified being totally ignored.

DeWitt W. Knapp
4921 Far Rockaway Boulevard
Far Rockaway, NY 10765
(718) 555–7746

February 3, 19--

To those concerned with data processing support:

As a tech/support analyst for the New York Stock Exchange's state-of-the-art DP center, my brain is my office. I carry the innermost workings of the equipment and its software in my head.

Our department's goal is always to maximize availability of the system to users by minimizing downtime. I must make equipment/data check corrections on DASD devices and carry out recovery procedures in the shortest amount of time.

For example, the exchange's batch processing is done overnight. If either the mass storage device or DASD devices malfunction, it can hold up a whole night's work. One night it nearly did, but I had it up and running in 20 minutes, without calling IBM for assistance, or looking it up in a manual.

I also have good written and oral communications skills. I explain new techniques or procedures to users. I also maintain them in a manual, and issue them in the form of written instructions. And at each morning's turnover meeting, I relate to the director the nature of any problems that arose overnight (hardware? software? applications?), what action was taken, and in what time frame.

I have just moved into a new home in New Orleans, which I had built for me two years ago because I plan to live here permanently. Perhaps you have a position in your own organization for a DP professional like me where my diagnostic skills will be valued.

Sincerely,

Note: The author chose a salutation broad enough to include just about everybody in a position to influence his hiring. His opening radiates self-confidence. Notice he mentions building a new home in the city he plans to move to — a positive sign of roots and permanence to a prospective employer. Unfortunately, I was unable to reach the writer before he moved to New Orleans to learn how well this letter did for him in pulling interviews.

Norman L. Devris
234 E. 89th Street/11Q
New York, NY 11206
(212) 555–1067

June 28, 19--

To life insurance agency presidents and sales managers:

If you have been wrestling with the problem of how to build your agency's profits in this recessionary market, my resume will hold interest for you.

Our general insurance agency is running much better since I joined it a year ago. That is not my opinion; it is a statement of fact: when I joined, I had about two dozen pending files. Now I have more than 300.

What made the difference is my calling licensed insurance reps, most of whom are not able to keep abreast of the many life products being offered nowadays, and offering them informed selling ideas and strategies to beat back the competition. I explained the advantages and benefits of 90% of the policies they are called upon to write.

I used the phone, direct mail, seminars and personal visits to their offices. Every time they turned around, there I was with tested solutions to their sales problems.

I wish to relocate to the Boston area and am seeking a position similar to the one I have now.

Perhaps you have underperforming accounts buried in your database that can have new life breathed into them. Let us work together to get more profitable ideas to your accounts and the accounts will solve the problem of how to build your future. I may be reached at (212) 555–1067. Thank you.

Sincerely,

> **Note:** A sure basis for attention is knowing the prospective employer's business so well you can talk to them in their own language. The easygoing manner of this letter is appropriate. Employers like being talked to assertively. Notice, no reason for the relocation is given. Alas, I have not been able to contact the writer to learn how well the letter pulled.

Wade L. LeMoyne Painting Contractors
205 N. State Street
Detroit, MI 48226
(313) 555–4000

November 7, 19--

Mr. Frank F. Milliken
President
Milliken Custom Builders
400 Fenimore Parkway
Detroit, MI 48127

Dear Mr. Milliken:

Are you fed up with being let down by painters? Then please take into consideration my request to be placed on your active bidding list:

Speed: For Miranda Construction—40,000 sq. ft. / we were asked to speed completion by two weeks as tenants were moving in early / raised 4-man crew to 15 / worked Saturday and Sunday / finished two days early / *at no extra cost to the contractor.*

Thoroughness: The above job was a *commercial* job that came out like a private job. No runs or sags, flawless painting, trim was finely cut, doors nicely brushed, etc. / Miranda hired us to paint their executive offices, and have given us five assignments in the past 15 months.

Custom Work: You might care to know how I would handle your request for custom paint mixed to match your client's specs. Here's one thing we don't do: we don't routinely open a gallon of custom paint and start painting. If 10 gallons of custom-mixed paint are needed for the job, we mix all 10 gallons together and stir. Our experience is that custom-mixed paints vary in tone and density, from gallon to gallon, and must be stirred all together to be uniform.

You will notice the focus I have placed on our relationship with Miranda Construction. I like to build enduring relationships. What I wish for when I ask

Continued

to bid for your work is an opportunity to find someone like you who respects *reliability*.

Do you sometimes feel scared at what painters will do around costly furnishings? We just recently painted a brownstone mansion on Park Avenue. Chairs in the living room, we were told, cost $2,500 each.

I did not feel a need to issue any special instructions.

I have recruited, trained and motivated these painters. They anticipate everything, and overlook nothing. And, being commercial, they are so much sharper and shrewder than the average house painter. The job went off flawlessly, and the owner is endorsing us for a commercial job.

You don't find perfection often in this world. But I put everything I can into my house painting to make it the best and most durable:

- I monitor your job personally, daily.
- When you are given a finish date, we are finished on that date.
- Our painters are trained to be meticulously neat.
- I use only Benjamin Moore paints on all assignments.

I have not dealt with costs except to say we regularly bid on and win corporate and city jobs—where the work is usually given to the low-cost bidder.

But, because you get less of a price, does not mean you get less of a paint job. My work is fully backed by guarantee and insurance. What you are bid is what you pay—there are no hidden charges or other surprises sprung on you while the work is going on. If I misjudge our costs, we swallow the difference. I will call you next week to meet you and see if we can be placed on your bid list for your next painting job. Thank you.

Sincerely,

Note: Here is a typical business-to-business letter intended to secure new accounts. Notice the plentiful use of devices to break up the text and make a two-page letter *look and seem* shorter.
- First page has extra-wide top and bottom margins to make the text seem shorter / a large body of text is shifted to page two.
- Devices include underline, italic, dash, listings, itemization, subhead.
- First page ends with an unfinished sentence / a time-tested device in multipage letters because a reader's curiosity is aroused.
- Examples are given to back up every claim of superiority.

Lawrence M. Gelfand
1252 N.W. 14th Street / Suite 1226
Washington, DC 05612
(202) 555–1400

July 19, 19--

Mr. John. F. McKennan, Sr.
Director of Human Resources
Clark Oil & Refining Corp.
1510 Fannin Street
Houston, TX 45601

Dear Mr. McKennan:

Why let soaring benefits costs give you ulcers?

I have focused on *why* human resources directors are losing sleep over the colossal costs of welfare/health/benefit plans they are burdened with, and I have smart ideas to offer you.

I have educated myself in the subject from beginning to end, and from the middle to either end. (I have a complete law library in my home, and a complete library of books on insurance.) I concern myself not merely with the gigantic costs of the benefits, but also with the vast amounts organizations spend *to do calculations and administer the plans*.

Item: For a Fortune 500 company, I created a quotation system, by state and zip code, for quoting premiums on a national level / premiums included load factors such as administrative costs, reinsurance, etc. / designed the computer software and spreadsheets for implementing the system. The system cut administrative expenses 35%.

I am seeking per diem consulting work with large organizations where my presence could make a real difference in slashing your benefits costs to rock bottom, and probably increasing your coverage without costing you an extra penny.

Having someone like me review your plan could make a real difference in your comfort index. I'll call you shortly to discuss a time suitable to you for us to meet. Thank you.

Sincerely,

Note: This writer faces head on a problem common to most human resources managers—then offers an easy, pleasant and profitable solution. An excellent approach for those wishing to sell their services for profit.

Frank M. Preston
40 Old Post Road
Wilton, CT 11024
(203) 555–4986

November 19, 19--

Alan P. Kirsch, M.D.
Memorial Medical Clinic
40-60 Northern Blvd.
Bayside, NY 10321

Dear Dr. Kirsch:

Perhaps you need a nurse/medical assistant or E.M.T. with my experience and qualifications.

During my five-year active duty tour in the U.S. Air Force, I received extensive on-the-job training as a medical technician in almost every area of medicine: from surgical wards to pediatric clinics; from geriatric clinics to emergency rooms.

I have a good rapport with patients, doctors and other technicians, which always insures smooth sailing in any department I supervise. That's why my units were named the outstanding units, worldwide, three out of five years.

But most importantly, I love nursing and am completely dedicated to my work. I'll knock myself out to make sure a job is completed well and I don't need constant pats on the back to keep me working hard.

If you need a medical assistant who is good under pressure, experienced and completely dedicated, I think we have something to talk about. Thank you.

Sincerely,

Note: The writer states the purpose of his letter in the very first paragraph. He then proceeds to match his previous experience to the requirements of the new position. His years of training by the Air Force and love of nursing were enough to persuade hospital administrators to at least talk with him. He got interviews and is presently working in a hospital.

Bernadette L. McGrath
15 Norris Avenue
Oakbrook, IL 12032
(415) 555–3132

April 15, 19--

Personnel Director
American Museum of Natural History
79th St. & Central Park West
New York, NY 12024-4192

To whom it may concern:

In reference to the advertisement in *The New York Times*, dated April 10, 1990, please find enclosed a copy of my resume for the position as Assistant Volunteer Manager.

I believe that my academic background, communication skills and supervisory experience qualify me for the above mentioned position.

I am anxious to meet with you at your earliest convenience to discuss employment opportunities at your museum.

Sincerely yours,

> **Note:** I felt a little before-and-after example here might stress the point I made in the first line of my introduction to this book: "There is almost nothing you can't do with a cover letter, yet most people choose to do nothing." Here is the writer's original version. It is a mere letter of transmittal, revealing very little about the personality of its author. On the facing page is a copy of the revised letter that brought interviews.

Changing Careers/Museum Aide

After

Bernadette L. McGrath
15 Norris Avenue
Oakbrook, IL 12032
(415) 555–3132

April 15, 19--

Personnel Director
American Museum of Natural History
79th St. & Central Park West
New York, NY 12024-4192

Dear Director:

I have been waiting for an opportunity like this to write to you. Please take into consideration my application for the position of "Assistant Volunteer Manager."

I feel I am truly well fitted for this position – by reason of my outgoingness, my knowledge of archival research, and my willingness to share what I know about the human race with other people. You will read in my resume I meet all the requirements mentioned in your ad, including a B.A. in Anthropology.

I have been fascinated by museums going back to my first bicycle. In 1986 I made a marathon museum tour of the Far West, visiting 15 museums in four cities in two weeks. What fascinates me about museums is their ability to preserve culture, to learn from it and to teach from it.

You might not at once see a connection between my present work – real estate title researcher – but it is there. I research family structures, read wills, see how property has been distributed through generations. It's investigative.

All that I can hope to do here is to introduce myself and express my strong interest in the position. I will call you next week to discuss a personal meeting. Thank you.

Sincerely,

P.S. I tell my friends anthropology is a *religious* hobby. They ask, "What do you do to practice?" and I tell them, "I ride the subways every day."

> **Note:** Here is a rewrite of the McGrath letter on the opposite page – using only principles and suggestions given in this book. The writer has added a touch of humor in her P.S. Employers like to see a sense of humor in prospective employees.

Thomas L. Hardy, Jr.
24 Greenwich Street / 7U
Hoboken, NJ 20117
(201) 555–9001

March 21, 19--

Mr. Leonard R. Burden
Vice President
Prudential Bache Securities
30 Broad Street
New York, NY 10013

Dear Mr. Burden:

At first (and even at second glance), my resume does not jump up and scream, "Account Executive!" Yet, there is a lot about me, which can't be covered in a resume, which may convince you otherwise. Let me explain. It needn't take us long.

I come from the entertainment field where less than 1% of professionals are able to make an adequate living. I was among that 1%.

I have acquired my Series 7 (92% on exam) and 63 licenses, so I know what will be expected of me as an account executive. At the most basic level, a stockbroker is very much a salesperson – and that means cold calling on perfect strangers. When it comes to cold calling, I can do it all day. Rejection does not faze me. I have a great deal of experience recruiting business from corporate clients of the music studios I have run. I am confident I can provide a payoff for the firm that gives me the opportunity.

They say stockbrokers work long, hard hours. After working 24 hours at a stretch recording and editing albums, I'm prepared for anything.

And when it comes to building a client base, I already have a head start. During my years as a professional musician and producer, I developed close personal relationships with many affluent members of the entertainment industry. I have a list of dozens of potential clients . . . all earning six-figure incomes . . . as well as hundreds of their friends and associates.

I would like to arrange an agreeable time to meet and discuss my potential to quickly become an asset to your firm. I will call you next week, or, I may be reached at (201) 555–9001. Thank you.

Sincerely,

> **Note:** One of the few exclamation points you will see in all these examples ends the first sentence. Note, also, the six-line paragraph is bordered on both sides by paragraphs of two lines . . . to keep readers from yawning at the sight of a massive block of text. The writer wrote me, "This letter was the key to opening up the doors."

Bonny M. Michaelson
14 Sutton Place South / 10G
New York, NY 11722
(212) 555–1264

March 14, 19--

Mr. William Dudley Sloan
William Dudley Sloan Real Estate Brokers
24 E. 58th Street
New York, NY 10019

Dear Mr. Sloan:

A major insurance company came upon a simple test whereby they could predict with almost complete accuracy the future success of new salespeople.

They asked each applicant for a sales position how much insurance he or she presently owned. Those who already owned insurance almost invariably had greater success in selling it than nonowners because the owners truly believed in the worth of what they were selling.

I have a very successful background in selling: most recently as president of Starlight Fashions. At Starlight, I introduced a patented product and built sales from zero to $5.5 million before the company was acquired. Prior to that I was president of Michaelson Construction, which specializes in interior renovations. I sold over 75 jobs, ranging up to $300,000. I know construction and quality. I know Manhattan. I know the rent control and building codes.

I am a persistent cold caller, and know how to qualify a customer. I never tire of prospecting. I have always had one foot in real estate investment and development (please see resume). I took money from my business to invest in real estate. I always made money. I am enclosing a list of real estate transactions I have carried out.

Now that I have sold my business, I want to go full time into real estate sales, which brings me to the point of my letter. Perhaps you have a sales position in your own organization for a proven performer like me – who meets the insurance company's rule-of-thumb test for future sales success.

I'll call you next week to arrange an agreeable time for us to meet personally. Thank you.

Sincerely,

Note: The writer relates her previous background to the requirements of the position she aspires to. This is the single most important element of a changing careers cover letter. When you are seeking a job in another field for which you have little formal training, *use the whole letter to stress the match* between you and the job you're after. (See Special Purpose Letters.)

Brian C. Stafford
23 Richmond Court
Staten Island, NY 11672
(718) 555–9200

December 23, 19--

Ms. Deborah H. McClure
Director
Daytop Village
32 W. 40th Street
New York, NY 10016

Dear Ms. McClure:

I have been a police officer all my adult life.

Now I would like to use the strength and talent I gave to law enforcement to developing character in adolescents and in assisting families in coming together, through the role of guidance counselor.

One of the things you learn as a police officer is, in prison more than anywhere, people need a reason to hope, and someone to believe in. Their need of hope is so great they will believe in anything. The experiences of someone like me might make the growing up experience easier and a lot less painful. I know how to listen carefully, unquestioningly.

You will read in my resume I have taken coursework in *all* the social sciences and graduated with a major in psychology. Perhaps you have a counseling position at the entry level in your organization where my background will prove an asset. I may be reached at (718) 555–9200. Thank you.

Sincerely,

Note: Where does motivation originate? Internally only? Or externally? The letter writer feels *externally*. The author said he got good results from this letter because the reader was able to *feel* the personality behind the writing.

Kurt S. Russell
1121 Ashcroft Lane
Stamford, CT 20430
(203) 555–3317

September 8, 19--

Dear sales manager:

I suppose I should answer the most obvious question first (when you see my resume): "Why do you wish to leave a career in a scientific field to enter sales?"

I thought I would like the work a great deal more than I do. It isn't challenging work – not to me, at least.

Sales *is* challenging, for one reason, just because it is so measurable. You have a chance at a new personal best daily. You not only compete against yourself, but against others; you even compete against those who performed the job before you. As you will see on my resume, I love sports competition, and it loves me. I know I am temperamentally right for sales, and I wish to demonstrate that right here and now.

While in high school, I got a job nights telemarketing a credit card. I worked the phones night after night, for a year, then I graduated and entered college. I have been told the burnout rate for cold-call telemarketing is six weeks to six months (if they finish the first week). It might be easier going with these salespeople if they realized they *have no choice*. How else can a company bring in *new* accounts except by never-ending cold calling on perfect strangers?

You're sure to have some dormant accounts that could be doing better. How much more could you be making from them if someone set out to prove something to you? Give me the chance to convince you. I may be reached at (203) 555–3317. Thank you.

Sincerely,

Note: Here, the writer's resume was all about science with very little about sales. The cover letter had to carry the burden of convincing prospective employers he had sales potential, and it did. An anecdote was used, and the writer got interviews. When you are just a few years out of college, employers are very indulgent about career changes, knowing it takes time for some to find out what type of work they really like (and dislike). Thus, the writer felt safe in using what he did not like to lead into what he did like, and why.

Anne Cheryl Schabert
155 W. 68th St. - 807
New York, NY 10023
(212) 555–0450

October 11, 19--

To those on the administrative side of the performing arts:

I could talk a great deal about myself as an actress/singer and about appearing onstage in leading roles of various productions at Lincoln Center, N.Y.C. But I'd much rather talk about what I am prepared to do for you as an administrative aide.

I set up systems and procedures that are flexible enough to meet changing objectives. I speed and simplify the process of organizing meetings and training staff. I cost-effectively manage your projects, from initial planning to evaluating results and preparing effective reports. *Plus*, I am extraordinarily effective on the phone, and in oral presentations.

Item: I am a trained editor and writer: wrote news releases, publicity, programs, program notes, letters, reports, policy papers.

Item: I organized and directed theatrical productions as well as organized and booked concert tours.

Item: I am a trained fashion designer and seamstress and have worked on props and designed costumes for the Manhattan Opera Theater and the Viennese Operetta Company.

Item: I arrange music / compose lyrics / teach voice / wrote opera synopses for "Stagebill."

Item: I relate well to people and can represent your organization as a speaker. I have spoken before groups of as few as 25 and as many as several hundred. I have been interviewed on radio and TV.

Ideally, I would like to find an administrative position in the performing arts, broadcasting or publishing. I will call you within the next few days to discuss this matter further. Or, I may be reached at (212) 555–0450. Thank you.

Sincerely,

Note: The writer sent this letter to the hidden job market only. She said she was invited in for numerous interviews – "even when they did not have a specific opening at the moment."

Martin H. Jain
43-35 Mountain Terrace Road
Mountainside, NJ 21377
(203) 555–1483

October 28, 19--

To managers desiring greater productivity:

Greater productivity – including pay-for-performance – is going to become the new religion in America in the nineties, and I want to become a part of it as a management consultant.

New systems have to be analyzed before they are introduced. They have to be taken apart to see how much profit they will yield the organization. That ordinarily requires charts and graphs and statistics, econometric modeling, all of which I am excellent at. It's the type of work I am looking for.

I will go to any length to collect data to analyze. For one research project, I contacted over 30 libraries. I then spent 12-hour days sifting through the facts to find anything useful, and wrote a five-page report on my findings.

Knowledge is progressing at an accelerating speed, always faster. I am enclosing letters from three of my Economics professors. I have demonstrated, to them at least, the capacity to absorb knowledge, implement it, and pass it along to others. Give me the opportunity to convince you in an interview. If I did only what is usual and customary for your clients, it would not be enough. Thank you.

Sincerely,

Note: The writer called me to say he got three interviews in two weeks, including Salamon Brothers and Stone & Webster. He said he had mailed 50 copies of his previous cover letter and resume and gotten zero. The chief difference between the two, so far as I could see, is the assertive tone of this letter.

Bert R. Easton

136 College Point Boulevard
Yonkers, NY 13624
(914) 555–1850

August 5, 19--

To the project supervisor:

If you're looking for an assistant project supervisor, you won't find anyone who is more dedicated to construction than I am.

I have been working on construction sites since I was 15 – mixing cement, slagging, carting bricks – whatever was needed. Everyday after school, I visited the site because I loved to watch the building progress.

I spent a year and a half in New York learning large-scale construction from the best. My courses at the N.Y.U. Building Construction Management Program were taught by senior operating executives from leading construction firms including Tishman, Morse Diesel and the Port Authority. I was introduced to all phases of construction management:

- Budgeting and estimating.
- Cost management.
- Planning and scheduling.
- Project management.
- Contracting claims.
- Managing and operating.
- Use of Lotus 1-2-3 and other software.

I can read blue prints, assist on R.F.P. preparations, report on costs, evaluate job progress and supervise employees. I am not afraid of hard work and will do anything I am asked to. I would like to meet with you and discuss how my experience and abilities can be of use to you. I may be reached at (914) 555–1850. Thank you.

Sincerely,

> **Note:** This recent graduate said he got many interviews with this cover letter – at a time when the construction industry in New York City had just about come to a halt. Once again, love of the work is the framework of a winning letter.

Recent Graduate

Roberto N. Reid
256 Ferndale Road
New Hyde Park, NY 11566
(516) 555–4341

May 17, 19--

Dear marketing manager:

Please take into consideration my request to be evaluated for an entry-level business position in administration or marketing. This is about me, but will interest you:

Fast learner: I started as a stockboy at Baldostri's Market while attending school (resume), but was quickly promoted to Assistant Manager when they found I could explain to customers the characteristics of all 125 cheeses stocked.

Fast performer: I worked as a teller at Chase Bank while attending school at night. Tellers are expected to process 150 transactions a day. I averaged 200 a day.

Exact: Had only one "difference" (when a teller's accounts do not balance at day's end) all year (30,000 transactions).

Dedicated: Did not attend my Phi Beta Kappa presentation ceremony because bank was short-handed that day.

Punctual: Had perfect attendance record.

Whenever a new teller was hired, I was selected to train them because I am very accurate, very polite, appropriately dressed at all times, and know how to get information. The bank noted in my performance review ". . . he is an asset to the branch."

I am more than willing to sell my future to a business organization for a chance to learn and grow, as I help you to grow.

Sincerely,

> **Note:** This letter fulfills every employer's two psychological hiring needs: (1) to stay safe, and (2) to look good. The writer told me, "Not only was I able to get interviews, but I got a very attractive job offer in my very first interview (later accepted) among other offers."

Jane F. Cavanaugh
24 Milford Circle
New Milford, CT 20312
(203) 555–1462

March 7, 19--

Mr. Alan N. Kaplan
Partner
Ridgewood, Kaplan, Fedlich, C.P.A.s
635 Third Avenue
New York, NY 10022

Dear Mr. Kaplan:

I thought I would lend more credibility to my request to be considered for a junior accountant's position if I began with what others have to say about me:

> "Ms. Cavanaugh broke important new ground in her thesis 'A Study of External Users' Perception of Financial Graphs.' Of all the students I have had over a 20-year period of teaching, she was one of the very best."
>
> – C.T. Lehman, Ph.D., C.P.A., C.M.A.
> Professor of Accountancy

Have you ever asked yourself, "How do external users – shareholders for instance – feel about the financial figures we accountants provide for their annual reports?"

We accountants, I feel, have an ethical obligation to be aware of the effect of our reporting on users of the information. Can the information be taken in quickly? Is it clear, unclouded and readily understood? Or does it conceal more than it reveals?

Theorizing about ethical considerations of accounting is important. But I would not wish it thought I am not equally concerned about the bread and butter work, the auditing and tax work. You will see in my resume I have passed the C.P.A. exam and am eager to join a public accounting firm as a junior accountant.

Perhaps you have a position in your own organization for a motivated worker like me. I am scrupulously exact and thorough in all my calculations, and will work earnestly to make you proud you employed me. Thank you.

Sincerely,

Note: This graduate uses the testimony of a college instructor to certify the quality of her accounting education. Many go to college to study accounting; not everyone learns.

Recent Graduate/Sports Marketing

Thomas M. Mannes
24 Kingston Drive
Larchmont, NY 10910
(914) 555–3541

July 12, 19--

Mr. Frederick H. Santos
Vice President Public Events
New York Knicks
Madison Square Garden
New York, NY 10022

Dear Mr. Santos:

Tell me, is there a greater high for players, managers and owners (and the vast public that clusters around them) than coming out the big winner at the season's end? I have known it (please see resume), and that is the whole point of my letter.

I know sports is also a *business*, and I intend to become a part of it and make it my career. If I had my druthers, everyone's dream is to work directly with the team. But I also know there are many other satisfying areas in sports-related marketing and public relations to which I could become devoted.

I feel a person like me — the sports enthusiast — can almost always perform with success in winning the public's favor. The enthusiasts are so soaked in sports they eat it, drink it and sleep it. An enthusiast will to go to any length to tell others of the happy feelings bubbling within.

Which brings us to the business part. I've mentioned in my resume several health-related events I took an active role in with visible success. Here's a work-related incident I did not mention, that will reveal my sales and closing skills:

I started at age 14 telemarketing subscriptions to the New York *Daily News*. I did it until age 21 — although I heard the average burn-out rate for telemarketers was four months. It was no problem with me. I believed in the worthiness of the *Daily News*. I expanded their readership, and took them into towns where they had never been before.

I penetrated Spanish-speaking neighborhoods for the paper. I had to be bilingual, so I learned Spanish. I won numerous sales contests, and a $150 cash bonus for a marketing idea.

The best I can hope to do in this letter is to present myself and to request an interview. I will call you next week to arrange an agreeable time for us to meet. Or, I may be reached at (914) 555–3541. A year from now, I will make you proud you took the trouble to interview me. Thank you.

Sincerely,

Note: Here a recent graduate with no experience at all in the job he is applying for has used a related accomplishment to show fitness for the job.

Frank R. Graham
234 Wisteria Boulevard
Pompton Lakes, NJ 23784
(203) 555–1483

July 20, 19--

Mr. Jack L. Abbott
Managing Partner
Consulting Group
Ernst & Young
240 Park Avenue
New York, NY 10022

Dear Mr. Abbott:

Business pays firms like Ernst & Young handsomely for problem-solvers, and I intend to count myself among them.

Here's a rather typical example of how I tackle a challenge just because it is there; running through the details needn't take us long.

The Business Club of the University of New York was a club in name only. It had no regular meetings, no record of membership, and fewer than a half-dozen members. It had existed thus for at least 10 years.

Held a competition.

I formed an executive committee, and we at once held a competition to rename the moribund club. We got about 40 suggestions, and the first prize of $25 went to the name Aspiring Corporate Executives Club, which everyone felt reflected the club's purpose.

I got a list of all business students, undergrads and graduate, and mailed them an invitation to come together in the club and share experiences. I spoke to previous members of the club and to the faculty for their input.

I paid personal calls on the town's business leaders and asked them how we business students could make ourselves helpful to the town, and how the town's business leaders could help us students to grow professionally. I also invited certain business leaders to be guest speakers at our meetings, which we held biweekly.

Continued

Membership rose to 20 . . . then to 30 . . .

We served refreshments ($1 for a drink and burger). I got there early to set up. Pretty soon we had 20 or more students at a meeting, then 30, then 40 or more. Dues were set at $15 a year. For one meeting, I organized a panel discussion on the trade deficit. I invited one of my own professors as well as a professor from another university.

As president, I replaced a vice president who was not pulling his weight. I spoke with the head of the business school about expanding the intership program. The school had presumed a lack of interest because only 3–4 internships a semester were arranged. Now, that number is 10–15 a semester. We raised $600 through a raffle and presented the business school with a TV and VCR. (I got Wal-mart and Sears to donate the raffle prizes of $100, $50 and $25.)

When I graduated last year, the Aspiring Corporate Executives Club had 50 dues-paying, meeting-attending members, with its own intramural volleyball team (placed second in competition).

I felt very fulfilled. I learned so much that I could never have learned in class about organizing, delegating, persuading.

All problems are simple to solve when you reduce them to fundamentals. It's the reducing that's difficult, and that is what I am truly well fitted for. Which brings me to my reason for writing you this letter.

You will read in my resume I worked for Peat, Marwick in a consulting capacity. I analyzed internal controls of Unilever, conducted a system study of Nestle Co., and prepared a report to management on a Japanese-Sri Lankan joint venture.

I am seeking an entry-level position with a consulting firm where I can grow into an expert whom companies and other organizations will hire and retain, and where my boss will be proud of hiring me. I am young and earnest and determined, and I plan to call you next week to arrange an agreeable time for us to meet. Thank you.

Sincerely,

> **Note:** I included this letter to demonstrate two-page letters do get read—so long as you remain interesting. The writer of this letter got interviews and a consulting job he loves, with a rather prominent firm. Subheads are used to break the letter into small-seeming parts and to sustain interest. The letter is built entirely around a school-related anecdote that shows the writer at his best. Notice the writer tells *how* as well as *what*. Because, in telling how, he *demonstrates* traits of character: persuasive, decisive (fired a vice president), team player (got more internships), and so forth. Employers say, "Don't tell me—show me."

Priscilla S. Sanders
23 E. 77th Street / 9E
New York, NY 11583
(212) 555–4588

October 24, 19--

Mr. Arthur L. Malone
Vice President Offshore Production
Cal-Tex Fabrics, Inc.
440 Broadway
New York, NY 10031

Dear Mr. Malone:

You may need a trainee in import/export with my management and educational background.

I have nearly one year of experience managing a department with New York City's leading department store. I have been successful in tackling some of the company's most important problems and have developed skills needed in every business: employee supervision and motivation / inventory management / recordkeeping / evaluation of sales performance and customer service.

Item: *Cut annual departmental inventory shrinkage from $100,000 to $25,000 in first year* (the store stressed this as one of their most pressing problems).

Item: *Improved departmental sales in eight out of ten merchandise groups* — achieved increases of up to 120%.

In addition to my current management experience, I have stressed international business throughout my education. I am fluent in French and majored in International Careers.

I quickly will become an asset to your company. I am not afraid of long hours and hard work, and know how to produce concrete results to add to your profits. Let's arrange a convenient time to meet so we can discuss my usefulness to your firm. I'll call you next Thursday. Thank you.

Sincerely,

Note: There are four devices from Chapter 7 used in this letter. It brought the writer interviews . . . and the position she sought.

Joseph R. Layton
451 E. 9th Street
Hartsdale, NY 11923
(914) 555–2621

March 17, 19--

Ms. Abbie L. Livingston
Producer
CBS Evening News
340 Avenue of the Americas
New York, NY 10022

Dear Ms. Livingston:

Need a desk or production assistant for your news department? Someone who has hands-on experience and extensive training in news production?

I have recently graduated from college with a degree in communications and have also completed an internship in the news department of ABC-TV.

I participated in many areas of news/televison production, including on-location shoots / studio productions / research projects / script preparation / use of BASYS computer system / and miscellaneous office duties.

News production is all I've ever wanted to do, and I'm eager to learn all I can while putting my skills and enthusiasm to work for you wherever you feel I am needed. I like challenges (resume) and look forward to any new project assigned to me. Given the chance, you will find I quickly become an asset to your newsroom.

If you need an assistant with energy, initiative *and* on-the-job experience, then we may be right for each other. I plan to call you this coming week to discuss a convenient time for us to meet. Thank you.

Sincerely,

Note: This letter has an effective feeling of ardor about it, communicating the writer's zeal to the printed page.

Clifford M. Daugherty
420 N. Leighton Avenue
Williamston, VT 08764
(802) 555–8901

June 12, 19--

Mr. L. Thomas Bolan
Senior Vice President
Real Estate Loan Group
Citicorp
65 Exchange Place
New York, NY 10013

Dear Mr. Bolan:

Suppose a developer comes to you for a construction loan for what he or she says is a can't-lose deal . . . for a highly marketable property . . . that will pay off its loan with ease.

With someone like me on staff, you could have usable facts like the ones I am about to mention right at your fingertips:

- Are the builder's construction costs reasonable, or are they over- or underestimated?
- Is the project feasible for the current market?
- Are the builder's assumptions ("it'll be 90% leased/sold") realistic?
- Is another project of this kind needed in proposed area?
- Are the prices expected by the developer reasonable in current market?
- How likely is the project to earn back its interest costs?

I'm not nearly through, but I think you get the point. I have learned how to get all sorts of usable facts and information. For instance, I called a large accounting firm for some lease and rental data on their four floors of space on behalf of a developer wishing to build an office tower nearby. "That's private," I was told, followed by a hang-up. So, I called someone else there who was in a position to know, and again got nowhere. I called a third time, to still another executive, and got the facts I wanted.

What I am seeking is an entry-level position in your real estate loan department. I was straight A in Accounting and Finance in business school. I know how to take a real estate balance sheet apart, and, as you can see, I am unrelenting in my research. If you like these attributes, then you will quite possibly like me. I will call you to arrange an interview, or I can be reached at (802) 555–8901. Thank you.

Sincerely,

Note: The writer was told at one interview, "Yours was the most fantastic cover letter I have ever read." The writer opens with a typical chancy situation the prospective employer is confronted with. Not to worry. Read the writer's tremendous third paragraph—the listing. It fulfills the employer's No. 1 requirement: hiring someone who can make me feel safe.

Recent Graduate/Sales

William K. Morrison
241 Charles Street / 14K
Hartford, CT 20312
(203) 555–4243

November 2, 19--

Dear sales manager:

Prospects' doors turned on their hinges when I called — slammed shut. I counted five turndowns for every sale I made.

I was selling advertising sponsorship on the college FM station to local merchants. Except our station — WICB-FM — is required by law and college policy to be commercial free. So we decided to sell sponsorships ("underwritings") of our programs, particularly coverage of our baseball, football and basketball games.

These underwritings gave the advertiser's name and a brief message about the nature of the business — similar to the Public Broadcasting System.

<u>My hardest sale.</u>

My hardest sale was to a dealer in antiques and oriental rugs, who felt college students were not his natural market. I had to call several times just to get an appointment. But we got him; moreover, he renewed.

Each student is permitted to occupy this position for just one year. During my year, I set an all-time school record of over $10,000 (the previous high had been $7,000). The money was used to buy equipment and supplies for the station.

Which brings me to the point of my letter. I am seeking an entry-level sales or related position in broadcasting, where my very excellent sales skills will prove effective in the heat of today's competition. I know how to read a rate card, understand the audience research systems, drive-time, prime-time, late-night, and much more. I have studied for this job for four years (resume), and I may be reached at (203) 555–4243. Thank you.

Sincerely,

Note: Campus activities which reveal your positive character traits are excellent subjects for cover letters. Your accomplishments become twice as impressive when you show you had to meet and overcome obstacles to achieve them. The writer told me, "Without the focus on my campus activity, I never would have gotten my job."

Allen M. Murphy
201 Amsterdam Avenue / 17J
Kearney, NJ 01786
(201) 555–0089

September 16, 19--

To those concerned with ship brokerage:

I recently received my B.S. in Marine Transportation and am seeking an entry-level position in the ship brokerage industry. I am willing to make whatever sacrifices it takes to succeed.

I am not looking for high salary and benefits; merely a chance to learn the industry and to make myself a credit to your firm. I propose to first deliver results, and then leave it to you to be fair about the reward.

I have some practical deck experience. I worked summers as a deck apprentice aboard freighters. I assisted with preparation of ship documents such as bills of lading, ship manifests, etc. And I have a good general knowledge of the function of the ship broker.

I know admiralty law / nautical rules of the road / shipyard operations / maritime cargo systems / seamanship and vessel operation / port and terminal operations / tugs and towing / firefighting and damage control / meteorology / celestial and terrestrial navigation / marine electronics / radar and radio navigation systems . . . and even ship's medicine.

I am going to school nights to earn my M.S. in Maritime Transportation, and desire to continue my schooling while working full time with you. I assure you neither my work nor my studies will suffer in any way; I am used to working while studying.

I am seeking a career position where I will continue to work even after I get my M.S. Perhaps there is a position in your own organization for someone like me who truly loves the sea and ships. Thank you.

Sincerely,

Note: Here is an example of a cover letter with no previous accomplishments mentioned at all. Yet, because of its earnest tone and the writer's strong work ethic, he got interviews and a job.

Recent Graduate/Assistant Editor

Roseanne D. Palais
44 Oak Street
Huntington, WV 51614
(312) 555–4359

December 12, 19--

Dear editor-in-chief:

Books are as important as bread to a small and devoted band of people, and I count myself a member of that band.

I therefore ask you to take into consideration my request for employment as assistant editor. I am well qualified academically and temperamentally. But you don't have to take my word for that. I will back up that statement with facts:

ITEM: I have trained myself to read over 1,000 words a minute. I go through a book like a person walking barefoot over hot coals—with haste.

ITEM: I can sum up a manuscript, estimate its chances, and explain my findings to you in clear, concise memos.

ITEM: I took a writing course from Mystery Writers of America, and am at work on a horror-story novelette. I like mysteries, sci-fi and horror stories so well written and plotted they can stand alone as straight novels.

ITEM: Passed New York University's English competency exam for graduate students on my first try.

What Aristotle said of drama is true of written fiction: The work must contain plot / character / theme / story / spectacle.

I have the talent, I have the knowledge, I have the skills, and may be reached at (312) 555–4359. Thank you.

Sincerely,

> **Note:** The opening invites the reader's interest, and the recitation of facts backs up the interest the opening has aroused. Another device mentioned in Chapter 7 is used in the final paragraph, i.e., repetition of key words or phrases, i.e., *I have the* . . . , to provide rhythm. The writer said she got good results with this letter.

Melissa M. Burton
40 Governor Dewey Parkway
Larchmont, NY 20311
(914) 555–0021

February 20, 19--

Dear sales manager:

Isn't this the type of performance you'd be looking for in someone you are considering for a sales position?

- Exceeded quota by 787% for 1991.
- Ranked No. 1 out of 14 salespersons in my office (ranked No. 2 out of 12 in previous position and named "Salesperson of the Month" five times).
- Continually realize 25% annual sales increases.
- Paid 100% of college costs through selling.
- Make up to 100 cold calls on offices weekly.

The whole point I am trying to make in this letter is that I love selling, and I believe I can sell *anything*. I feel that, so long as you possess the basic selling skills and you brush off rejections like Teflon, all needed product knowledge can be learned.

I am seeking a sales position where I can set more records and make my manager proud of hiring me. Just give me the chance to convince you in an interview. I may be reached at (914) 555–0021. Thank you.

Sincerely,

Note: This letter writer wrote me, "Human Resources was very impressed with my cover letter and within three weeks I found the job I wanted." Often you may be told, "Avoid sending your cover letter and resume to Human Resources." Don't you believe it. It's their job to keep an eye open for worthy applicants. And when they forward your letter to the person doing the hiring, you have their implied endorsement of you. (Of course, if you can discover the name of the hiring person, send directly to that person.)

Bank Assistant Manager

William K. Marshall
1345 47th Place
Chicago, IL 31207
(403) 555–3798

July 3, 19--

Ms. Kathleen N. Nisbet
Director of Human Resources
First State Bank of Chicago
33 Michigan Avenue
Chicago, IL 30016

Dear Ms. Nisbet:

Teller desertions after brief periods of employment cost banks tens of millions a year, and every bank is looking for an escape.

At our headquarters branch, many tellers have been here for three to five years, and one or two for as long as I have been here (eight years).

Our customers are watched, listened to, waited on (and spied upon . . . our branch has had only one fraudulent transaction slip past our tellers in eight years).

How do you get tellers to complete transactions speedily, learn quickly, be enthusiastic toward customers and—*stay put*? How do you bring down the time needed for a teller to perform any transaction, and have no problem employees who give you Excedrin-type headaches? You might send for someone with my love of the work.

I am seeking a position as executive assistant, or as a trainer, in a bank immensely larger than my present employer, with a faster tempo and greater challenges, preferably international in scope.

I can have nothing but pleasure, I am sure, in hearing of any opening you may care to discuss. I plan to call you next week to arrange an agreeable time to meet. Or, I may be reached at (403) 555–3798. Thank you.

Sincerely,

Note: Again, a writer spotlights a humongous and recurring problem of the employer's, and offers to solve it once and for all. For that kind of benefit, an employer *makes* time to go on reading: "Maybe this person really can solve my problem."

Veronica L. Burke
47 Thomasville Avenue
Trenton, NJ 20217
(203) 555–1140

July 11, 19--

Mr. Roger E. McGuffey
Chief Lending Officer
First New Jersey National Bank
30 Broad Street
Trenton, NJ 20482

Dear Mr. McGuffey:

Have you not found that granting loans so often involves a knowledge of accounting and the law?

For instance, I rely on my accounting background completely to read my way through often tangled financial statements presented by prospective borrowers. Likewise, my comprehension of the legalities governing lending in New Jersey permit me to carry out corporate and consumer lending activity safely; namely, collection.

I have recovered $6 million in bad debts since 1979. I have time-tested techniques that bring to terms even the most obstinate, resistant debtors.

But, first of all, I have tests I put to prospective borrowers to determine credit worthiness. I hope you will agree with me, if this part of the loan transaction is attended to scrupulously, little need will exist for collection procedures.

My philosophy for approving credit lines is to extend just the right amount, and no more. If they have less than they need, they cannot run their operations. If they get more than they need, they will perhaps invest it elsewhere than indicated. I also research for possible hidden costs that the borrowers perhaps have not calculated in their selling prices, as well as how well suited the borrowers are to accomplish their projections.

I am seeking a position in corporate lending where my knowledge of law, accounting and banking will be of great and immediate use—and will make a true difference in the operating results. I may be reached at (203) 555–1840. Thank you.

Sincerely,

Note: "You incur little risk in hiring me . . . I apply tested banking principles . . . and success comes," is the message here. Please note the paragraph in bold italics. Sometimes, a single ability is valued by the employer far above others. This letter was written during a period of deep recession, and the writer thought the ability to collect past-due debts was worth emphasizing.

Company President

Anthony S. Warren
40 Coventry Court
Short Hills, NJ 21453
(201) 555–7546

January 25, 19--

Mr. Dwight D. Everett
Chairperson
New York Bank for Savings
23 Park Avenue South
New York, NY 10018

Dear Mr. Everett:

You may be interested in this brief account of how I made a very lucrative mortgage transaction for my company in 1991 . . . when the real estate vacancy rate reached a new high . . . when money for this type of transaction was hidden away awaiting better times.

In 1991 a large developer converted 10 buildings with 3,300 units and a sell-out price of $900 million. "The premium mortgage deal in New York City," one newspaper article called it, and I went after it. I . . .

- negotiated the deal in five meetings.
- made the pitch / wrote seven-page proposal, including all boiler plate.
- secured *two* lenders (Guardsman Life and First National) . . . in a bad market, when there was very little money around for this kind of transaction.
- persuaded Guardsman to waive their entire presell guidelines and to relax their product qualifications for second homes.

We beat out two big money center banks and several mortgage firms for this deal. The developer has since come to us with a second deal on 220 units.

I have developed a mortgage product for employers of fewer than 250 employees that makes all three parties happy: the *employee*—who has a desirable employee benefit that offers substantial savings / the *employer*—because the company now has a desirable employee benefit to offer that costs them nothing / and, of course, the *broker*.

Perhaps you have a spot in your own organization for a peak performing deal producer like me who has never failed to break sales records wherever I have worked. I will call you next week to discuss an appropriate time for us to meet. Thank you.

Sincerely,

Note: This letter is crawling with devices: the dash and ellipses, bullets, underline, italics, direct quotation—all intended to keep the reader reading longer.

Bernard H. Hermin

40 Pearl River Avenue

Pearl River, NY 32145

(914) 555–8900

March 21, 19--

Mr. Harold F. Pohlson
Vice President
DRL Air Freight
Dock 40 / Kennedy Airport
Queens, NY 11565

Dear Mr. Pohlson:

You probably have hidden profits in your business that a remarkably thorough manager like me could uncover.

* *Increased sales from $90,000 a month to $125,000 / gross profit margin is up 17% through efficiencies I introduced.*

* *Introduced system — later adopted by all 10 company offices — of sending stacks of faxes by computer / saved $10,000 a year per office.*

One of the easiest ways to increase profits is to attract motivated workers. And teach peak performance to those already on the job (I believe peak performance can be taught and learned). I make regular walk-throughs of our office and warehouse. It's not just to let the staff know I am observing them at work, but to let them know through praise that I appreciate their contribution. It also allows me to spot potential problems before they occur.

I like to measure performance and keep management informed: I furnish a P&L to headquarters every Monday morning and actual income and expenses vs. budget. Thank you.

Sincerely,

Note: At one of his interviews, the writer of this letter was told, "It shows executive level thinking." All that is meant by that remark is the writer has addressed some of the chief concerns of every business executive: *profits, cost cutting, above-average employee productivity, keeping management informed,* etc.

Manager/Retail Toy Store/Novelty Format

Bruce A. Solomon
410 E. 79th Street / 11E
New York, NY 11314
(212) 555–3485

March 7, 19--

Director of Personnel
Dept. NE 56
Lionel Kiddie City
2951 Grant Ave.
Philadelphia, PA 19114

Dear Director:

The job of managing—or assisting to manage—your new Queens toy store suits me admirably, and vice versa.

Let me prove that to you. I show on my resume where I meet six of the six requirements in your ad. Lord knows, accomplishments like those are not rarities with me.

I am going to add another proof, which I did not include in my resume. I like this next example because it shows clearly why I believe I am well suited to this position.

1974–80 **Store Manager**
The Train Store, New York, NY
(The Train Store is a chain of toy stores in New York City)
- Managed 34th Street store (three levels), supervised two others.
- Wholesalers confirmed my store was the largest seller of toy trains in the city.
- 34th Street store had volume of $500,000, two others $200,000 each.
- Bought all bicycles and did repairs.
- Handled store design, windows, interior and holiday displays.
- Shopped toy fairs to find hot new products.
- Built custom train layouts for customers. This service was so popular, two assistants were hired to do only this.
- Had whole floor devoted to train layouts.
- Built a 60′ train layout as the central display of the floor.
- Selling toys brings feelings of gladness through me all day.

I will call you later this week to set an agreeable time for us to meet. Or, I may be reached at (212) 555–3485. Thank you.

Sincerely,

Note: The novelty format was chosen because the specific toy store experience was far down on his resume chronologically (1974–80), and he wished to spotlight it. Once again you can see the versatility of the cover letter vs. the resume. The writer responded to a large display ad, but did not feel a need to mention it right off. Employers know their ads are running. He got the interview and the job.

James E. Torres
4120 Chambers Avenue
Bayonne, NJ 20451
(203) 555–7800

January 28, 19--

Mr. Vito L. Antoniazzi
General Manager
Stella D'Oro Company
41 Bronx Terminal Market
Bronx, NY 11432

Dear Mr. Antoniazzi:

I have increased sales and profits, and had the lowest labor costs proportionate to sales, of any store manager in Food Town's history.

Moreover, I did not have to coax, coerce or clobber the 50 employees in my store to team with me to set that record. I led them to it by working alongside them, explaining, listening and guiding. I used all the proven ways to get people to buy your ideas and support you. I got them all to become superstars of customer service. (Four of them have gone on to become store managers.)

I built sales, also, by stocking products most wanted in depth, and by discontinuing slow movers that did not earn their keep.

I left Food Town to become a route salesperson for Tropicana (resume). I at once organized the route to cut deliveries from five days to three, allowing me to make more cold sales calls on new accounts. I categorized the retail accounts by sales volume, paying the most calls on the most important. I doubled the route's sales from $3,000 to $6,000 a week.

What I am seeking now is a management position with a retail grocery chain, wholesaler, or manufacturer seeking more shelf space, and more sales. I feel I will be an excellent manager or salesperson because I am an excellent goodwill builder — I know how to talk the retailer's language. And I know the retailer's problems, hopes and goals.

I feel sure — I am sure — I will be an asset to your organization in bringing in new accounts and getting more sales from existing accounts, and I may be reached at (203) 555–7800. Thank you.

Sincerely,

Note: *Leadership* is a trait much sought-after by employers. This writer does not merely *claim* to be a leader, which any cover letter writer can do. He cites a concrete example of his leadership skills.

Manager/Building Superintendent

David S. Rosario, Jr.
125 E. 135th Street / 12X
Bronx, NY 13117
(212) 555–1375

October 22, 19--

To those concerned with building maintenance and renovation:

One of the first things I learned when I became a building superintendent was this: Buildings are run for the purpose of returning a profit to the owner, but the illusion must be sustained among tenants that the building is being run exclusively for their safety and comfort.

So you will find me very tenant-and shareholder-focused. Tenants are quick to panic. They panic because they feel helpless. One of the ways I reduced tenant stress to a minimum when I was superintendent for 55 apartments, was to leave my own door open night and day. It was never locked. Tenants could walk in, explain their problem, and I would tell them, "When you come back tomorrow, it will be fixed."

In addition to tenant relations, I operated a gas and oil boiler / operated the compactor and kept it clean / installed sinks, stoves and refrigerators / repaired dryers, air conditioners and washers / installed kitchen cabinets / made small roof repairs / performed preventive maintenance on boiler and other equipment / replaced light fixtures, locks, broken glass in doors and windows / bought needed supplies and equipment.

I made the building a safe, lovely, clean place to live or work. I give tenants no reasons to leave and many to stay put. I am able to maintain good relationships at every level: with people I work for, the people I work with, and the people who work under my direction. And all my references are excellent. Thank you.

Sincerely,

> **Note:** The ability to *read* people — to size people up and know what they are thinking and feeling — is an amazing skill. And when you say you can read the people critical to the success of your prospective employer's business, your words will be read. The writer said, "I could not handle all the interviews, and I finally got the job I have been seeking for some time."

Milton R. MacAndrews
5621 Peachtree Road N.E.
Atlanta, GA 33427
(404) 555–3921

May 9, 19--

To those in charge of warehousing and distribution:

I have a dirty fingernails education in warehousing and distribution.

I have performed every single function in working my way up from the bottom to manager — from working in the shipping/receiving departments to buying equipment and recommending software programs to increase efficiency.

Perhaps that is why I have been able to motivate and get the most out of people and reduce costly turnover, even with the very low entry wage and minimal benefits that are often found in warehousing.

I have cross-trained the entire staff to perform each other's work when one or another is out. We have 25 people, but we get out such great quantities of merchandise every day that we have become the third biggest U.P.S. shipper in New York City. I did not let that fact pass unnoticed. I negotiated with U.P.S. for a 10% discount. I don't have the space to recount here how I did it, but I can tell you it took eight months of negotiation with eight separate U.P.S. executives.

Our company is relocating out of state in early spring. I am seeking a warehouse management position where I can put my successful strategies to work to improve morale / slash waste / improve accuracy / and enhance customer loyalty through speedier service. I may be reached at (404) 555–3921. Thank you.

Sincerely,

P.S.   I have taken (and passed) a polygraph test, have excellent references, and am bondable. This is important when you control a $1 million inventory, as I do.

Note: The writer promises to put an end to unwanted warehouse turnover and save you money too. The P.S. is an excellent clincher. The writer reported "a lot of favorable comments about the letter from interviewers."

Michael Johnson
241 Escadrille Drive
Lakehurst, NC 56189
(508) 555–9234

October 7, 19--

Mr. Gilbert M. Howe
President
Howe Controls Manufacturing Co.
14 Route 27 N
Marietta, GA 40434

Dear Mr. Howe:

How many of these common motivational problems do you find among your employees?

Lack of cooperation? Repeated absenteeism or lateness? Frequent breaks? Resentment of authority? Slovenly record keeping? Missed deadlines?

I presently supervise a staff of 12. But I feel the tested principles I apply to correct bad work habits and behavior can just as readily be applied to 1,200.

I wrote a training manual that spells out clearly everything new hires need to know about what is expected of them. I go over assignments personally rather than by memo. I explain what is wanted—and what is not wanted—so employees can make the most efficient use of their time.

The result has been that average project turnover in our office has been slashed from 2–3 weeks when I arrived to 72 hours. We constantly finish assignments ahead of schedule, and under budget. My boss has gotten letters from some of our biggest accounts expressing admiration at the speed with which their projects were completed. The firm's income has increased 60% since I have been Director of Operations.

I am seeking a position as operations manager or supervisor where my abilities to deliver better results than were expected will be valued. I may be reached at (508) 555–9234. Thank you.

Sincerely,

Note: Here is an example of an opening that asks a question that cannot be dismissed with a simple yes or no. It sets up a train of thought in the mind of the reader that leads directly into the body of the letter.

Luis M. Garcia
124 N. W. Highland Avenue
Arlington, VA 22206
(703) 555–1300

April 24, 19--

Dear fast-food restaurant owner/operator:

Three characteristics have made me a successful manager: my ability to
1) motivate employees, 2) prepare successful promotions and 3) keep everything
running like clockwork.

Most recently, as general manager of a Burger King, I applied my expertise
and instincts to significantly increase sales in an industry where it is difficult simply to
stay even.

I did this by maintaining a highly efficient top-notch staff that I recruited and
trained myself.

I also implemented many promotional schemes that kept customer flow at a
maximum. These included offering tour bus drivers free meals to encourage them to
bring their tours here for lunch. I kept in constant contact with local hotels and planned
coupon discounts whenever large tour groups checked in. One coupon promotion was
so successful, it increased gross sales on the products involved 2% (ordinarily, discount
promotions lose revenue).

You may need a management supervisor with my energy, initiative and
experience. Let's arrange an agreeable time to meet so we can discuss how I can quickly
become an asset to your organization.

Sincerely,

P.S.   I did not mention it in my resume, but you perhaps would like to know that I
        was selected by Burger King whenever they opened a new store. I usually
        worked at the new store for a week or so to make sure the staff was properly
        trained and could deal with the volume. I opened at least a half-dozen stores.

Note: You should consider the P.S. an integral part of your letter,
even though it appears to be only an afterthought. Save a really important accomplishment or distinction for your P.S. because it is always one of the best read parts of a letter. Some readers skip right
to the P.S., then read the rest of the letter.

Barbara J. Gerard
16 N. 41st Avenue / 20 L
Teaneck, NJ 21753
(203) 555–1237

August 13, 19--

RE: M64406 WWD

To those involved with sourcing:

Several things you said in your ad for a professional sourcing executive make me think you may be searching for someone with my experience.

I have sourced virtually all of the international apparel-producing countries. Moreover, I personally visited each of the countries.

Our factories turn out some extremely fine workmanship; it sometimes surprises people. One of the contributing reasons is I write an operations manual for each factory. They have the standard set in concrete right there in front of them. There are instructions for every phase of the production process, from placing the product label to handling documents.

Because you are involved in sourcing, you know improperly prepared/delivered documents are one of the biggest sources of headaches and delays. I have a comprehensive knowledge of the customs regulations and documents for each of the 18 countries on my resume.

Incidentally, I did not mention it on my resume, but I was a paid consultant on foreign trade for the Commerce Department, and lectured to American manufacturers in Miami, New York and Boston on exporting to foreign countries.

Overseas sourcing requires a knowledge of each country you must acquire, and a talent for negotiation you must possess. Neither is common, and both are essential. Because I cannot call you, I may be reached at (203) 555–1237. Thank you.

Sincerely,

Note: The writer of this cover letter faxed me this message: "Just a note to let you know that I was one of four people interviewed for this position out of 46 who responded to their ad." When addressing a box number, create a salutation appropriate to the position applied for.

Thomas R. Corcoran
459 Yellowstone Road / 4J
Queens, NY 11404
(718) 555–1185

January 5, 19--

Dear building owner/operator:

You may need a superintendent with my qualifications.

Most recently, I have been working as a mechanic and assistant super in a large residential building and am familiar with the maintenance of all building systems. These include steam, air conditioning, plumbing, electrical and other routine maintenance.

In addition to my knowledge of building operations, I have worked for seven years as a warehouse supervisor where I developed the record-keeping and common-sense business skills required in a superintendent to manage the affairs of a building.

I was in charge of all billing and supervision of deliveries and managed to greatly improve the efficiency of the warehouse. With White Front Meats, I saved our largest account ($30,000/month) by talking a client into reinstating our products.

My two most important qualities are my ability to relate well with the tenants and my dedication to my work. The superintendent at my current position congratulated me on my ability to get along with the tenants and make them feel comfortable talking with me.

And when it comes to working, I have always been available when needed. I realize being a superintendent is a 24-hour-a-day responsibility and have no reservations about taking it on.

Let's arrange an agreeable time for us to meet so we can discuss how I may be useful in keeping your building running well. I can be reached at (718) 555–1185.

Sincerely,

Note: The writer said he got interviews and a job, and then loaned his letter and resume to three friends to use in writing their own.

Chief Financial Officer

Rebecca A. Simmons
127 Elm Street
Holyoke, MA 02319
(714) 555–0960

April 1, 19--

Mr. Marvin F. McGurn
President
Charleston Mills
Charleston, SC 80177

Dear Mr. McGurn:

In today's savagely cutthroat business environment, the finance office must become a profit center like everybody else — to aid the company in becoming a low-cost operator. At least those are my sentiments.

For instance, my cash management generated over $30 million available for investment. Income generated from this cash hoard was at one time the biggest profit center in the company.

Similarly, I review benefits carriers constantly. By converting to least-cost quality carriers, our company avoided the 30% general increase in benefits costs most companies have had to endure during the past five years, <u>and kept benefits costs constant</u>.

Our sales have grown from $10 million to $120 million. I took the company public and obtained a N.Y.S.E. listing.

Being the low-cost operator is becoming the new religion of the nineties. Financial officers like me can earn their costs back doubly and triply. I wish I had the space to demonstrate that to you here and now with example after example. But I will call you next week to arrange an interview (or I may be reached at 714–555–0960). Thank you.

Sincerely,

Note: As you read through these examples, I hope you do not tire of hearing of promises to lower an employer's costs — because employers never tire of reading or hearing about it. It is a subject of inexhaustible interest to them.

Franklin M. Garcia
99 146th Street / 8L
Raleigh, NC 38536
(515) 555–1231

May 23, 19--

Ms. Lydia N. Buckholtz
Office Manager
Tri-State Olds/Buick, Inc.
New Britain Road at Route 110
Raleigh, NC 37213

Dear Ms. Buckholtz:

What I am about to relate to you next is not an everyday occurrence in anyone's accounting department. I mention it here only to make a point: Nothing can take the place of thoroughness in accounting, even in this age of the computer.

While working for a large auto parts distributor, I discovered a $140,000 embezzlement from the company by my predecessor. I went back through past months of bank records on my own initiative, because they had been poorly reconciled. It was then I discovered suspicious transfers, and the defalcation was brought to light. Criminal charges were filed by the company.

I often work alone without supervision. For instance, I recently handled a state audit for a major tobacco wholesaler that took three weeks. The audit went back to 1981 (I started work in 1989). Nevertheless, I pieced together all the records needed, dating to 1981. The auditors said my work was "cooperative and helpful." No assessment was made, and the returns for those years were accepted as filed.

The whole point I wish to make in this letter is I am a very dedicated professional, very thorough, very exact. *Because I love the work*. Perhaps you have a position for a full-charge bookkeeper in your own organization, who is well grounded in all the basics of keeping a perfect set of books. I may be reached at (515) 555–1231. Thank you.

Sincerely,

Note: Here, not one but two work-related incidents are used to show the writer as someone who contributes to his employer's success. Employers believe *previous* accomplishments are the best forecaster of future success.

Chief Financial Officer

Nathan F. Pedersen
1 Luckie Drive
Greenwich, CT 08461
(203) 555–3299

July 30, 19--

Ms. Robin Hanover
Gray, Harbison, Walker Associates
Executive Recruiters
1601 Pan Am Building
New York, NY 10016

Dear Ms. Hanover:

Several requirements mentioned in your ad for a Group Financial Manager suggest you may be seeking someone with my background:

ITEM: "Previous experience in the Middle East"—I was C.F.O. of one of the major engineering companies in Lebanon, with $40 million in fees. I also worked for two years in Kuwait (page 2 of resume).

ITEM: "Liaison closely with MIS"—Over 20 lines of my resume are devoted to MIS accomplishments in developing systems for financial/accounting, marketing, production, distribution.

ITEM: "Masters Degree in Finance and Accounting"—Yes, with concentration in international business administration.

ITEM: "Working across all finance functions"—Solid experience in cash management, foreign currency transactions, acquisitions, public company, credit lines, bank borrowings . . .

. . . I wish I had the space to list it all here. But I think you see the fit. I am presently employed, but the prospect of returning to the Middle East is attractive to me. Because you prefer I not call you, I may be reached at (203) 555–3299. Thank you.

Sincerely,

Note: When you want to answer an ad, consider using your cover letter as this writer has—to match your abilities to the ad's requirements, *and establish your suitability for the position.*

Burton N. Grant
7 Old Greenwich Road
Greenwich, CT 21302
(203) 555–7100

October 4, 19--

Mr. J. Raymond Thornton
President
Amco Industries
200 Route 17
Millbrook, NJ 20117

Dear Mr. Thornton:

As the chief financial officer of a company, you receive scores of charts, tables, memos, reports and print-outs.

But buried in the reports also are calamities poised to happen. For example, for a consumer packaging business I vetoed a proposal to build a $35 million plant to double capacity when research showed the capacity was unneeded.

In an earlier instance, I was sent as controller to a money-losing packaging plant, a high-cost, union operation, and a big headache to the company. I came up with a plan to compress production into three weeks of the month, and close the plant the last week. As soon as feasible thereafter, the plant was consolidated with another plant in another state — all part of the strategy I set up to handle this loaded question of what should we do?

You will read in my resume of my positive side — how I raised millions of dollars for a start-up company and guided it to profitability and a public underwriting. I can provide scores of other examples.

I can respond to any financial or operating situation likely to arise in a company — from installing a complete financial and MIS system to taking the company public. I will call you next week to arrange an agreeable time for us to meet. Or, I may be reached at (203) 555–7100. Thank you.

Sincerely,

Note: The chief financial officer is among those in any organization in a position to directly affect profits — often by merely saying "No." We have talked a lot about accomplishments as the heart of a cover letter. But don't ignore the importance of shooting down someone else's bad idea. It shows keen business judgment and *decisiveness*.

Controller

William P. Saez

44 Kissena Drive / 16H
Flushing, NY 11355
(718) 555–3153

February 2, 19--

Mr. Howard M. Miller
Chief Financial Officer
Calvin Klein, Inc.
400 E. 57th Street
New York, NY 10027

Dear Mr. Miller:

Baron Rothschild was supposed to have said, "I would not give five minutes listening to someone tell me how to make $1 million, but I would stay up all night listening to how I could keep from losing $100,000."

Closing a department or whole plant, and putting unneeded workers out on the street, is very disagreeable work. Ask me—I have done it three times. But since when has putting an end to senseless company extravagance stopped being one of a controller's responsibilities?

Some of the things you said in your ad make me feel you are searching for a controller with my experience. My background matches all of your requirements. I write reports that get your attention. I install information systems that can access every bit of information critical to your business. Systems I have designed let you plan ahead and even project the future on a day-to-day basis. They also save time . . . minimize errors . . . provide answers to critical questions . . . reduce returns . . . measure performance—all in 10% of the time it took to perform these tasks before.

I believe I can perform in this position to your complete satisfaction, and I may be reached at (718) 555–3153. Thank you.

Sincerely,

Note: Business executives know waste and losses can more readily be cut than new profits can be made. Cost cutting—a strong, basic, emotional appeal to *any* employer. You'll see it repeated again and again in these examples.

John Frantzen
4001 Eastern Parkway Extension
Norville, NY 11415
(914) 555–1192

July 7, 19--

Mr. Herman R. Leyland
Managing Partner
Herman R. Leyland, C.P.A.
505 Fifth Avenue
New York, NY 10021

Dear Mr. Leyland:

One of the first things I learned in my present job dealing with high-net-worth clients in the entertainment industry is *money goes where it is well treated*.

My firm's clients require a *lot* of attention; they're used to it. The tact of a diplomat is as much of a requirement as knowing how to calculate with precision their world-wide royalties, paid in a variety of currencies.

You will read in my resume I am accountable for many, many responsibilities. I like having a lot of responsibilities. Without extra responsibilities or problems, a job could get boring. Despite my heavy burden of responsibilities, I have never missed a deadline.

I am seeking a position as full-charge bookkeeper where my comprehensive knowledge of the entire bookkeeping function will bring you the results you are looking for. I will call you shortly to discuss a personal interview. Thank you.

Sincerely,

Note: Promising an employer that customers/clients will get kid glove treatment is always pleasant reading in a cover letter. This writer received his first of many interview invitations one hour from the time he faxed the letter and resume to an employer.

Patricia J. Swanson
21 E. 78th Street / 14N
New York, NY 10055
(212) 555–5840

July 10, 19--

Mr. Ben W. Macalennan
Managing Partner
Smythe, Kukauer, Lloyd & Kimble, C.P.A.s
440 Third Avenue
New York, NY 10023

Dear Mr. Macalennan:

You will read in my resume I have supervised massive audits / computed taxes and prepared tax returns / drafted letters and opinions / and certified balance sheets. But that is not nearly all. *Every* competent senior accountant does those things.

I also advise clients on investing profits to minimize taxes / analyze their product lines and determine their true operating costs / forecast the profits each line needs to contribute to reach future goals.

Something else you may care to know about me, I have formal education as a corporate secretary. I perform all the functions—from setting up a company to reporting to shareholders. Thus, I can inform company officers and directors of their obligations under their own bylaws and the laws of New York State.

I am seeking the position of senior accountant where the diverse skills above described will be of great and immediate use. I may be reached at (212) 555–5840. Thank you.

Sincerely,

Note: The writer of this letter answers the question "Why are you the best person for this position?" That is all any cover letter can hope to accomplish, and this one got the writer many interviews.

Jennifer L. David
58 E. 94th Street / L10
New York, NY 11552
(212) 555–3711

February 22, 19--

Mr. Cyrus H. Gelb
Partner
Leventhol & Co.
30 Broadway
New York, NY 10012

Dear Mr. Gelb:

When I was about to graduate from Lehigh in Accounting, I said yes to one of the firms that interviewed me on campus and went right to work and was happy.

Then an event occurred at our firm that surprised everybody: Our third-biggest account has decided to do internally the work I was principally involved with.

But I crammed a goldmine of practical accounting experience into 10 months. (I also had time to coordinate the firm's blood drive and its offer on Channel 5 News to prepare taxes free for people affected personally by the Gulf Crisis.)

I worked in close contact with managers and gained exposure to many areas. On the third-largest account above mentioned, I worked with about 40 lawyers on their trusts, P.C.s and so forth. I became comfortable working with high-net-worth clients.

Very-high-net-worth clients are interested in calculations of their tax liability in the same way as athletes are concerned about their X rays. I worked out projections of future liability on B.N.A. software. I worked out what-if scenarios, showing advantages and disadvantages of paying taxes in the present or in the future.

I used Solomon to update expenses and general ledger and to produce trial balances and financial statements. I am, of course, familiar with Computax and Fastax, including transmission by modem.

Perhaps you have a position for a junior accountant like me in your own organization. For your convenience, I will call you next week to arrange an agreeable time for us to meet. Or, I may be reached at (212) 555–3711. Thank you.

Sincerely,

Note: Usually, but not always, the reason for leaving your last position is not given in your cover letter. This writer wove it positively into her letter, implying the firm parted with her services only when they were forced to. She got several interviews and was quickly re-hired.

Accountant/Senior/Seeking Per Diem Work

Walter B. Wrightsman, C.P.A.
2749 S. Powdermill Boulevard
Jacksonville, FL 33755
(305) 555–1264

November 10, 19--

Mr. Samuel J. Elias
Spitz, Port & Hall, C.P.A.s
Southeast Bank Building
Miami, FL 33245

Dear Mr. Elias:

I could write a book, certainly a pamphlet, on the ways operating executives have of kidding themselves about their true costs and underpricing bids.

The commonest error is not including includable items. And it is surprising how little time this analysis takes. I have made something of a specialty in analyzing business costs, as you will read in my resume.

I am analytical by nature, and this is one of the reasons why I am attracted to per diem work, now that I have had a taste of it. There are so many fresh cases of underpricing out there to be discovered. This kind of information can be worth a fortune to a company, and a feather in the cap of the accounting firm that furnishes it.

I offer knowledge and experience in virtually every accounting function a C.P.A. firm is called upon to provide. Moreover, I get the job done. The work does not go on interminably for long, long months, without resolution. Give me an assignment, and it gets done.

The accountant can provide an important service in increasing a company's profitability, and I provide it at moderate per diem rates. I may be reached at (305) 555–1264. Thank you.

Sincerely,

Note: The prospect of being able to furnish information "worth a fortune" to a client got the attention of a lot of accounting firms, and the writer got all the per diem work he could handle.

Pauline L. Winston
41 Poplar Street
Pound Ridge, NJ 23104
(201) 555–0117

August 13, 19--

Ms. Helen N. Wills
Creative Director
Gorden, Bowen & Purvice Advertising
22 N. Route 40
Philadelphia, PA 12462

Dear Ms. Wills:

My comprehensive experience in graphic arts production can help you cost effectively manage your production budget—cut your preparation time—and sometimes save as much as 25% on your printing.

You will see in my resume how often I make one dollar do the work of three in buying printing and four-color separations. I am a professionally trained photographer. I often take pictures for ads myself. I can save you hours of time in selecting models, setting up shoots, choosing a location, choosing a theme, photo supervision and editing.

A rundown of some of my other skills needn't take us long:

- Innovate graphic and photographic techniques to create new looks.
- Prepare conceptuals, comps, mechanicals.
- Supervise and approve duotones, half-tones and veloxes.
- Exceptional at creating innovative themes for ad campaigns.
- Liaison with vendors and clients / keep clients happy and coming back.
- Excellent at specing type.

The best I can hope to do in this letter is to present myself and my skills, and request an interview to show my work. Balzac said, "The guest is a better judge of a feast than the chef." I may be reached at (201) 555–0117. Thank you.

Sincerely,

Note: The art director always works as part of a team; nevertheless, there still are ways to distinguish oneself. Here is one of the suggestions in this book that holds true in *any* possible situation. It applies equally to businesses run for profit, as well as not-for-profit: *The offer to reduce an employer's costs of operation will never fail to win favorable attention.* One interviewer told the writer, "Your letter has all the right ingredients."

Patternmaker

Wilma D. Ratner
128 Beach Boulevard
Coney Island, NY 24407
(718) 555–3178

August 24, 19--

Dear apparel manufacturing manager:

I meet and in some cases exceed the requirements in your ad for a patternmaker. Let me demonstrate that for you right here and now:

Requirement	Wilma Ratner
"Must make first patterns from design sketches."	First pattern is made flat, draped or knocked off. Make two or three patterns a day depending upon the details of the sketch.
"Organized."	Classified and numbered filing patterns. Set order of priorities for samples and patterns.
"Speed."	Salesperson may have buyer in showroom who wants garment duplicated right away for meeting next morning. No problem. Used to emergencies, rushes, and so forth.
"Work with samplemakers."	Work now with three samplemakers. Instruct them in construction of garment, invite them to ask questions, let them study the garment. Often sit down at machine and demonstrate.
"Know denim."	Know denim weights, washing instructions, and able to calculate shrinkage. Experienced in stretch denim and twill.

I am a patternmaker with knowledge of all the elements that go into manufacturing a garment. I know I can perform to your complete satisfaction, and six months from now you will congratulate yourself for having taken the time for a short personal interview. I can be reached at (718) 555–3178. Thank you.

Sincerely,

> **Note:** This format shows the wonderful capability of a cover letter to match an ad's requirements with an applicant's abilities. Otherwise, the prospective employer is left to fish out the details in the resume when the resume only is sent.

Alexander M. Braun
128 E. Orchard Street / 12N
Hackensack, NY 21330
(203) 555–5260

September 28, 19--

Mr. George F. Kennen
Executive Vice President
Vogue Fashions, Inc.
1440 Broadway
New York, NY 11613

Dear George:

I've been thinking of what else I might do to line up new business opportunities, and I thought it would be very sensible to send you a copy of a resume I've prepared.

You will read in my resume I emphasized my two strongest qualities: as a production executive with comprehensive business and plant management experience, and as an executive with thorough knowledge of the federal government procurement process.

I built the plant, bought and installed the machinery, hired all the necessary workers, bought yarn and fabric, scheduled production — and brought finished garments to the marketplace. I also had a design department to create garments, and I positioned, priced and distributed them.

I have equity capital to invest if you know of a situation; or, I am also interested in landing a management position with a company that can utilize my in-depth experience. I am looking at any and all opportunities, and no situation is beneath my notice. Looking back, I have brought a great many profitable items to the market and helped a lot of companies make a lot of money. I plan to do so again and will welcome any input you can furnish. Thank you.

Sincerely,

Note: Seventy-five percent of all jobs are gotten through networking — writing to friends, business associates, friends of friends . . . anyone in a position to possibly help you locate a job opening in your field.

Networking/Special Purpose Letter

Blanche Rosen
215 Robinston Street
Pittsburgh, PA 15217
(412) 555–0138

November 15, 19--

Ms. Rachel Wade Harrison
Director of Public Information
CBS Network
430 Avenue of the Americas
New York, NY 10022

Dear Ms. Harrison:

Your name was given to me at a University of Pittsburgh alumni meeting by Joan Danziger as someone who could perhaps help me get a leg up in the public relations industry.

I am seeking an entry-level position, of course, but I already have experience in some of the needed skills. For instance, as a public relations intern, I wrote product publicity <u>that got picked up.</u> I wrote factual news squibs for periodicals to use to fill unbought space. I told people how to clean aluminum siding / install asphalt roofing yourself / build your own cedar home, and so forth. News clips came back showing 10 periodicals had picked up these releases.

Here's another skill I developed. I was nicknamed "Mannix" for my detective work in nailing down data about celebrities or other accounts the principals of the agency wished to pitch.

I also help to set up press parties. Our client's film was chosen for screening at a fund raiser. I . . .

. . . handled reservations / called guests to confirm if not heard from.
. . . greeted guests / brought hosts and artists to the parts of the room where press was waiting.

I am enclosing a copy of my resume and plan to call you next week. I will very much appreciate any insight, guidance, tips or suggestions you may feel inclined to provide a recent Pitt graduate. Thank you.

Fraternally yours,

Note: Many colleges publish handbooks giving the names, occupations, addresses and phone numbers of alumni. These are intended specifically for use in networking. Most alumni are willing to give of themselves to other graduates of their alma mater (Latin, *nourishing mother*).

Maurice LeClerc
4221 N.W. 121st Street
Miami Shores, FL 33446
(305) 555–7834

June 12, 19--

Dear restaurant owner:

If restaurants had numbers for names, the restaurants where I have been executive chef would still have identities — which cannot be said for scores of others.

For instance:

Item: *Le Caravelle*, where I am *chef de cuisine*, would be called 2½ — the number of stars by which it is now rated (before I came, it had none).

Item: *Michelle* restaurant, where I was also *chef de cuisine*, would be known as 3rd — because Madeline Boulé wrote in the Miami *Herald* "*Michelle* is the third finest restaurant in South Florida" (out of several hundred restaurants).

Item: *Jean's* would be known as 100, because it was listed by the *National Restaurant Owners* magazine among the 100 most profitable restaurants in the United States.

Not only have these restaurants been runaway successes, but they got ahead quickly. With *Le Caravelle*, the restaurant reached its full seating capacity within the first six months.

Moreover, these restaurants not only have had money success, but social success as well. You will read in my resume that celebrities such as Frank Sinatra, Elizabeth Taylor, Marlon Brando and others patronized these restaurants when they were in the vicinity.

I am interested in obtaining a position as executive chef in Florida or Hawaii, and may be reached at (305) 555–7834. Thank you.

Sincerely,

> **Note:** The before-and-after contrasts can be quite effective in telling of your accomplishments. You see it used here in the first "Item," and also in many of the examples in this book. The writer said he got a job offer in his first interview, and in subsequent interviews.

Dylan M. Masterson
415 S. Ellsworth Avenue
Detroit, MI 36431
(465) 555–1986

June 30, 19--

Dear human resources director:

Breakthrough sales opportunities keep popping up all the time. But you might not expect a technician to be the one to find them.

For instance:

ITEM: *For a major bank* — The bank's leased equipment was malfunctioning, the bank was complaining . . . and the bank's lease was running out. I traced the source of the problem, persuaded them to retain the present equipment <u>and buy a second.</u> I also identified a problem they had with someone else's equipment — they are replacing it with our equipment, <u>and a service contract.</u>

ITEM: *For one of the city's bureaus* — They had our outdated equipment. While repairing some of it, I evaluated their future needs. They are now negotiating for $1 million of our newest equipment.

ITEM: *For a major brokerage company* — I went there on a service call and discovered they had a $40 million DP deal on the table with IBM. They were not aware our equipment can interface with IBM. A $500,000 contract for *our* new equipment is now being negotiated (plus they saved $80,000 they had intended to spend on a consultant).

These are not just random occurrences. I wish I had room to list them all in this letter. The whole point I am trying to make is I do all in my power to see my company succeed. I pass sales leads on to the sales department as soon as I sniff one out on my service calls. (I am extremely knowledgeable about what our competitors are offering, and I am expert in connecting one manufacturer's equipment to another's.)

Perhaps your own organization has a place for a superb computer technician like me who earns his costs back just by providing sales leads for the marketing department. Thank you.

Sincerely,

Note: This letter merely demonstrates that *every* employee can make a contribution to the organization's success. This technician, over and above doing his analyses and repairs superbly well, found time — and the inclination — to gain valuable leads for the sales department.

Calvin J. Hunt
214 E. 75th Street / 12R
Trenton, NJ 07104
(212) 555–4508

March 16, 19--

Ms. Hanna M. Schriver
Assistant Executive Director
Housing Authority of the City of New York
New York, NY 10011

Dear Ms. Schriver:

Several things you said in your ad for a Director of MIS make me feel you are searching for someone with my background.

I have created systems for many of the most needed applications in any organization's daily operating routines (please see resume). So, I'd like to mention another feature from which you will greatly benefit; namely, my attention to users.

Unless the people who are to use the new system understand, approve and accept it, you could wind up benefit rich with productivity little changed.

My strategy is to get employees involved before and during the project, always pointing out its advantages to *them*. I take nothing for granted. I write the user manual at a 9th or 10th grade reading level. It is often advisable to consider a Spanish-language version. I hold classes. I bring the fastest learners along as fast as they can grasp the principles; and I never lose patience with the slowest learners. I delegate to some employees (the fastest learners) special responsibilities for the new system.

The position you advertise certainly is an excellent opportunity, and I want to throw my hat in the ring right now. I will call you shortly to arrange an interview. Thank you.

Sincerely,

P.S.   Incidentally, not everyone writes *documentation* when a project is done. I do. Without documentation, future enhancements of your new system(s) could cost you double—you'll pay for covering the same ground twice.

Note: This writer correctly judged that the prospective employer might be having a problem in training users. (He was right and got the interview.) The P.S. is used to offer a solution to still another very costly computer problem.

Computer Consultant

Paul B. Burton
1055 Lee Circle N.E.
Atlanta, GA 41563
(404) 555–0467

March 7, 19--

Mr. Claude H. Levitt
President
Levitt Consulting Group
240 Park Avenue
New York, NY 10022

Dear Mr. Levitt:

"The mark of a good consultant is to get renewed," said the president of a large DP consulting company in a recent issue of *Fortune*.

I worked as an outside DP consultant to NYNEX (of which New York Telephone Co. is a subsidiary), for eight years. My work made it possible for NYNEX to cut its run time by 50%, enabling a 70% reduction in staffing needs.

At one time a general rate change was done every eight years, required 30 staff and it took them 48 hours. As a result of my systems, it now can be completed in 20 hours, using nine people. During this time, I gave constant training to the NYNEX programmers in COBOL and IMS, in which the new systems were coded.

I sat in on meetings with upper management to make recommendations as to the viability of proposed projects. I advised on budgetary considerations, hours of code writing needed, amount of computer time for testing, equipment (e.g., to implement a system, NYNEX may have to buy three new disk drives), personnel/training needs (e.g., present personnel may not have needed expertise), and so forth.

I discouraged ideas that were not cost effective. Or, I advised postponement of a project because this was not the right time to get involved.

I am seeking a full-time consulting position in MIS. Perhaps you have a place in your own organization for a consultant who gets renewed through a steady flow of profit-aiding suggestions.

I often come up with an original approach to a project that offers an added benefit no one else had contemplated (please see "Error-Messaging" in resume), and I may be reached at (404) 555–0467. Thank you.

Sincerely,

Note: Here is yet another long letter that got interviews *by offering a benefit the prospective employer is known to prize highly* — a consultant who gets renewed. Notice how the writer closes with a strong benefit.

Nancy L. Jamison
234 Oak Avenue
Boston, MA 31436
(402) 555–6544

May 20, 19--

Dear data processing director:

For a chain of retail stores, I took an honestly awful system serving the headquarters and stores with very limited benefits and transformed it into a system ten times more effective (resume).

I have programmed systems to provide data on many essential management functions. And I have done it in every instance without a mentor or senior programmer looking over my shoulder. I just figured things out from the manuals because there was no documentation to guide me.

I am interested in an entry-level position in your computer systems department where my very excellent education in computer science, previous programming experience in applications software, and problem-solving abilities will give me a fast head start.

I learn fast—you won't have me coming back to you constantly with a lot of questions. Give me the chance to convince you I can make a valuable contribution, and earn my cost back several times over. I may be reached at (402) 555–6544. Thank you.

Sincerely,

Note: The statement "earn my cost back several times over" exudes self-assurance. (And her resume lists examples where she had done just that.) The writer also makes a point of being a rapid learner—two important benefits for an entry-level job applicant to offer. They brought her interviews and a job.

Concierge/Hotel

Jason A. Pettibone, Jr.
42-24 Beach Avenue / 2
Chicago, IL 11305
(405) 555–1351

August 6, 19--

Mr. David Pearlstein
General Manager
Palmer House
140 State Street
Chicago, IL 23104

Dear Mr. Pearlstein:

I am quite often asked to fulfill unusual requests from our hotel's guests (as well as field the general information questions that I get on a regular basis).

One such request involved a wedding party and a photographer that were staying with us. Both had stored rolling racks of clothing in our storage space. The wedding and the photo shoot were to happen on the same day.

Apparently, in the confusion, the rolling racks were switched. The bride had gotten bathing suits instead of her bridesmaid's dresses. The wedding was to begin in three hours on the North Shore and the photographer was on the South Shore somewhere.

While not neglecting my other duties, I managed to calm a bride . . . stall a wedding . . . find a photographer . . . within my three-hour deadline. The wedding went smoothly, only fifteen minutes late.

I am applying for the position of Guest Services Agent. The hotel industry has fine-tuned the extensive customer services skill I have already learned in retailing. I look forward to challenge — and 110% is not enough. If you are looking for someone to sell your hotel's services while doing it credit, you will find in me someone uniquely qualified.

Sincerely,

Note: Again, the work-related anecdote pulls response. Notice how the writer uses one paragraph for each idea. Readers like things made easy for them. The letter also looks easy to read *physically* — with its five short paragraphs. The writer said he sent this letter and his resume to seven hotels (in the hidden job market) and got five interviews.

George L. Atterbury, III
61 Bayside Court West
Phillipsburg, PA 10247
(215) 555–1294

September 19, 19--

Ms. Marge Howes
Human Resources Department
Johnson & Johnson, Inc.
Parsippany, NJ 20138

Dear Ms. Howes:

Please take into consideration my request to be considered for the position of Johnson & Johnson's Facilities Management Director.

Perhaps I ought to say right here at the start *I have never exceeded a budget nor a completion date in my entire career.*

Other abilities of mine that deserve special mention in these recessionary times: 1) ability to renegotiate contracts downward with vendors (resume), and 2) thorough knowledge of environmental laws—city, state and federal (resume).

You will see in my resume I have undertaken and overcome every problem or situation likely to arise in the running of a huge, modern office tower.

For instance, I was asked by the owners to draw up a proposal to merge our building with an adjoining building. I drew up a plan that was to the mutual benefit and *satisfaction* of both building owners. Negotiations are now underway.

The owners refinanced a building six years ago and had to put money into an escrow account for asbestos abatement, required by the lender. I was given the task of preparing all the paperwork for submission to the lender, verifying full compliance with all regulations as a condition for the escrow money being released. Funds were released as scheduled.

If you'd like your building to run as smoothly as a Rolls Royce, I'm someone who can accomplish it. I'll call you next week to arrange a suitable date for an interview. Or, I may be reached at (215) 555–1294. Thank you.

Sincerely,

Note: Six of the seven paragraphs in this letter are merely two or three lines. Your reader may be tired or just lazy, and short paragraphs *seem* less intimidating to the eye than do paragraphs of eight or ten lines . . . when a letter is picked up to be read.

Customer Service

Santos R. Santana, Jr.
35 Laurelton Street / 12M
Houston, TX 79127
(821) 555–0976

February 14, 19--

Mr. Hobart F. Galbreath
Vice President of Operations
Trans-Tex Pipeline Co.
4215 Gatewood Drive
Houston, TX 78213

Dear Mr. Galbreath:

Joe Pearl urged me to contact you about a position in your large customer service department, and I do so with the greatest pleasure in the world. Who wouldn't like to belong to the Trans-Tex organization?

Here's my attitude toward customer service: Out of complaints and problems, good things can grow for a company.

In fact, I often considered writing a little booklet on the opportunities presented to an organization when a customer voices a complaint. I look at it this way. Keeping customers happy after you've sold them can make even more money for the company. For one thing, there is loyalty—they'll think of you before they'll give business away to an outsider. For another, they may not be as price sensitive, valuing service more than least cost.

I wouldn't want you to think I focus only on handling complaints. My present company held a contest to sell service policies. I sold 46 contracts over a 3-month period. Contracts were for $60 to $2,000 a year. I earned $1,600 in commissions (it would have been $3,200, but I split 50/50 with the field representatives).

I am nicknamed "The Answer Man" because I know all of the company's products (3 product areas, about 25 products each, with 10-20 accessories for each). This product knowledge permits me to be poised and confident in dealing with inquiries from our customers and prospects.

Perhaps you *do* have a place for me in the Trans-Tex organization—a young man with vision, who believes the customer is the reason for all the rest of us being there. Thank you.

Sincerely,

> **Note:** Please note the conversational tone of this letter—as if the writer were speaking face to face with the employer. Note, also, the emphasis the writer places on having a deep belief in the importance of his position, amounting almost to a credo. Note, too, the reference to his nickname, "The Answer Man." *Hint*: If your fellow workers have not assigned you a nickname, assign yourself one if you feel you deserve it. (The nicknames used in this and other examples in the book are actual.)

James J. Lemonyne
45 Lakehurst Drive
Pompano Lakes, FL 02154
(305) 555–2346

May 5, 19--

Personnel Director
Florida Racing Association
Hialeah, FL 33019

Dear Director:

Perhaps you have a position in your organization for someone whose resume "Profile" can be summed up in just five words: *The customer comes before everything.*

I start out with the notion that the customer is real and vital and sane, and our reason for being here. On my most recent job, I conducted customer-satisfaction audits (resume). I personally handled complaints from major customers. I was also placed on special assignment to find weak spots in the company's customer service programs.

Your track has concentrations on employees – 100 parimutuel clerks, 50 groundskeepers, 65 ushers, etc. These great cadres of people have great potential for spreading goodwill, without it costing you a penny extra. Let me demonstrate to you the ways to do it. I can be reached at (305) 555–2346. Thank you.

Sincerely,

Note: This letter and resume was sent to several race tracks and brought the writer interviews and a job. Employers know the customer comes before everything, but it takes strong incentives and bonuses to employees to keep *them* thinking that way.

Dentist

Felice A. Giliotti, D.D.S.
301 Old Boston Post Road
Boston, MA 60711
(617) 555–3144

January 18, 19--

Dear doctor:

Several things you said in your ad make me feel you may be searching for a dentist with my experience and background.

I have comprehensive experience in virtually all areas of general dentistry, with specialized experience in endodontics, prosthodontics and cosmetics. You will see in my resume I also fit in comfortably in every type of practice socioeconomically, from business people and professionals in midtown Boston and Cambridge, to blue collar, working class in Braintree and Roxbury.

I have taken several dozen postgraduate courses to learn more about specialties, and also about the business end of running a practice. I have taken courses at Harvard and Temple, and management seminars in New Jersey and California. I have taken a variety of Sterling's courses in internal marketing, external marketing, learning how to get patients to recommend other patients, building patients' confidence so they can commit to a program of necessary work, appointment control, and so forth.

I take these courses because I feel I want to stay current and enhance professional knowledge, so important nowadays. And because I believe no dental practice that wants to have a future can overlook the down-to-earth sensible advice from experts on management techniques needed to build successful practices. I may be reached at (617) 555–3144. Thank you.

Sincerely,

Note: Again and again, knowing the prospective employer's problems, hopes and aspirations is a sure way to inspire confidence and get noticed.

Barbara Ann Hollander
1220 Ash Avenue
Forest Hills, NY 11557
(718) 555–1367

February 5, 19--

Mr. Joseph P. Bowen
Vice President—Russ Girl Division
Russ Togs
140 President Street
Long Island City, NY 11254

Dear Mr. Bowen:

A whole army of top-earning designers are going to work to make you rich, but you will need to add only <u>one</u> designer's salary to your payroll.

"What's the catch?" you may well ask. There is no catch. You and I stroll by the fine and tony Madison Avenue specialty shops. Some item will catch your attention, and I will make a mental note, then come back with my sketch pad and draw it. Then magically I will transform it into a look-alike for *manufacturing at your price point.* You don't have to invest a penny.

But the role of the knock-off artist is more resourceful than *creative* and *innovative*, which I also am. I *create* 250 new designs a season for my present employer. I also created a hand-painted T-shirt program that was a big winner. Moreover, I am versatile: I create designs for children, missy and junior. And I design across all price lines.

At your fingertips, you will have the hottest source of fresh ideas a manufacturer could ask for. For your convenience, I will call *you* next week to arrange a suitable time for us to meet. Or, I may be reached at (718) 555–1367. Thank you.

Sincerely,

Note: What do you do when you can't *measure* your accomplishments? Because of its unceasing flow of benefits to the employer, this letter has remembrance value—even though the writer has not given actual sales figures for her designs.

Facilities Planner

Elizabeth M. Wright
420 Watermill Lane
Plainfield, IL 40712
(315) 555–3356

October 21, 19--

Mr. Lemuel C. Culver, Jr.
Director of Human Resources
Allstate Insurance Co.
450 Michigan Avenue
Chicago, IL 40211

Dear Mr. Culver:

As a Facilities Planner, I am called upon to provide tested solutions to problems <u>before</u> they arise.

But I was nominated for an award for my solution to a problem <u>after</u> the facility was completed. A brief description needn't take us long.

The architects of a 165-bed private nursing care facility for a religious organization provided a sit-down dining room that *accommodated only 100*. Patients were required to eat in three seatings.

I took part of an adjacent corridor, which faced an exterior atrium, and designed counter seating for 65. This addition reduced the seatings from three to two and permitted nurses to watch the added dining area without additional staff.

I was nominated for a "Practice Planning" award given by IFMA (International Facility Managers Association).

I begin every project with an exact and definitive needs analysis. I anticipate every situation and provide clear-cut guidance. Perhaps you have a need in the widespread offices of the Allstate organization for a facilities planner with my background.

I will call you next week to discuss a time for us to meet personally—and to show you several other facilities problems presented to me for solving. Thank you.

Sincerely,

Note: This letter demonstrates ability to focus on a problem . . . interpret data . . . and recommend strategy. Winning awards or other recognition for work well done is the work equivalent of making the Dean's List at college, and is an excellent subject for a cover letter.

Philip J. Katz
154 Glen Falls Avenue
Farmingdale, NY 11704
(516) 555–5163

July 10, 19--

Mr. William A. Gates
President
Olsen Temps
2340 Broadway
Hempstead, N.Y.

Dear Mr. Gates:

Nothing makes a room full of job applicants in gray flannel suits look so much alike as concentrating on the suits instead of the applicants.

If you view the job placement industry as a whole, you may fail to discover the qualities possessed by a few dedicated individual placement specialists like me.

I have experience sitting on both sides of the desk: the employer's side, and the recruiter's. I have placed people in the hundreds, and *90% of them are still there as I write this*. I brought in as new accounts two of the city's biggest banks.

On the client side, I moved swiftly to cut by half the hiring cost of temps. I have seen from the placement side how much money is allowed to dribble away by inept or lazy recruiting practices.

I attribute my 90% success rate in placing workers who stay put to the following:

– candidly explaining to the applicant the pros and cons of the position.
– you cannot hire *only* the people you like.
– don't hire only in your own image.
– check references thoroughly.

I am seeking a position as employment recruiter with an organization where my experience will be valued. I am a good judge of character and can expertly qualify people on the phone – fast! I'll call you next week to arrange an agreeable time for us to meet, or I may be reached at (516) 555–5163. Thank you.

Sincerely,

Note: Strong stopper opening, adaptable for many uses when you wish to show differences between you and your competitors. *The capability to reduce staff turnover* is a cover letter topic that again and again is inevitably right to catch an employer's attention. The writer said she got four interviews almost immediately, and the job she was after.

Exceptional Worker

Robert M. Fredrick
214 MacAllister Place
Far Rockaway, NY 12834
(718) 555–1735

April 19, 19--

To warehouse managers and supervisors:

This letter will introduce Robert M. Fredrick, who works for me. This facility will move to Virginia the first of the year. Staff has already been cut from 35 to 17.

Robert has worked under my supervision for over a year, and I have had a chance to observe his production and work habits.

He has not been absent a single day. He has not been late for work a single day. Nor was he ever late in returning from lunch. Moreover, Robert is ve-ry strong. Our facility receives and ships bales weighing 60-75 lbs. I have seen Robert throw one of these bales eight feet.

He is tireless and unperturbed about doing repetitive tasks that bore most other workers. For instance, he is part of a team loading and unloading 40′ trailers (we get about 10 a day). He does not take breaks, unless the others do. He does not drink, smoke or use drugs, and has a clean record and a driver's license (he used to drive a school van).

Although he is white, he has no problem working side by side with minority employees, a few of whom are tough street thugs on parole. His co-workers used to tease him, but when they found he only smiled with them, they gradually tired of the practice and accepted him.

Robert's weakness is he does not present himself confidently in interviews, and prospective bosses draw wrong conclusions. Too often the reverse is true, I have found: Job applicants come over strongly in the interview, and know all the appropriate answers to tough questions. Once on the job, they are just as adroit at goldbricking. Robert is able and steady, and will value the opportunity you give him far more than many others who are only better talkers.

I recommend Robert unreservedly to any warehouse or distribution center manager, and suggest you utilize him in those areas of fairly repetitive functions where he can keep going flat out all day without tiring or being bored. Every warehouse or distribution center needs people like Robert Fredrick.

Sincerely,

Note: Nowhere in the letter is it mentioned Robert is mentally retarded. He was told not to mail this cover letter, but to take it to warehouse managers in person for an on-the-spot interview. He got a job he likes after the second interview, with a higher salary and greater benefits, in a large company.

Helen W. Doud
245 W. Seneca Avenue
Los Angeles, CA 51372
(608) 555–5130

March 7, 19--

Box ABP-T95
4220 La Cienega Blvd.
Los Angeles, CA 10017

To those conducting the human resources director search:

Several things you said in your ad for a Director of Human Resources suggest you may be considering someone with my background.

I have wide experience on both sides of the desk: in securing jobs for people (I placed 75% of one school by graduation) / and in finding people for jobs for organizations (I was in charge of personnel administration and recruitment for a company with 7,000 employees). I have recruited personnel from entry level to executive / on college campuses and through classified ads / union and nonunion.

A few words about a subject worth many.

Another qualification I bring to the position is the facility to interact with and respect employment candidates at all levels. A large firm felt they were underrepresented by minorities in middle management. I conducted a search to find promotable minority candidates. I spoke with their supervisors who were resistant. Result: more minorities in middle management, and improved morale among the 1,750 unionized employees.

Surprisingly little is mentioned, however, about saving money in the personnel area. But one of the bigger, constant savings I have managed is developing sources for new hires where no fee has to be paid.

My experience and critical judgment will bring you the kind of faithful employees you are looking for, and quite possibly at less cost than you may now be bearing. Because I cannot call you, I may be reached at (608) 555–5130. Thank you.

Sincerely,

Note: A subhead is used by this writer to break up two longer paragraphs . . . and to arouse enough curiosity to propel the reader into the next paragraph. Notice the writer has used the work-related incident as a vehicle to display herself as a problem-solver and morale builder . . . plus a cost-cutter (fourth paragraph).

Laboratory Assistant

Mark L. Horovitz
31 Ferncliff Road
Wyandanch, NY 11723
(516) 555–0987

May 6, 19--

Dear laboratory director:

I am able to respond to any lab request, know all lab procedures, and can perform virtually every lab test with skill, conviction and speed.

I have been praised by my superiors for dedication to my outstanding patient care and for getting along harmoniously with all other members of the health team. At the Newark Hospital Center, I was interviewed for an article in the hospital newsletter.

I not only perform tests, I also prepare reports summarizing the test results for the use of the examining physician. I perform the whole range of procedures: urinalysis / occult blood in stool / pregnancy / sperm count / complete blood cell count / sweat test and the stool fat test. I am also familiar with all lab diagnostic equipment, what it is used for, and how to maintain it. I have worked with infants and children, adults, and geriatric.

I supervise three lab assistants, and I train them in procedures and use of lab equipment.

Perhaps you have a place in your own laboratory for someone like me who is educated for lab work, trained in a lab, and at home in the lab. I have been caught up in lab work since I was a small boy, and I may be reached at (516) 555–0987. Thank you.

Sincerely,

Note: As you skim through the examples, you will find salutations such as this one: *directed to the person who will be your boss.* Although nothing beats looking up each prospective employer's name, title, address, etc., for a highly personalized salutation, *impersonal* salutations like this one will not get in your way if your letter is absorbing to the reader. As a general rule of thumb, here is the order of precedence in addressing your cover letter: 1) the person likely to do the actual hiring, by name and title, 2) the company president of a very small company (250 or fewer employees), 3) the head of the department in which you will be employed, 4) the human resources department.

Carol J. Sternberg
245 Gresham Lane
Scarsdale, NY 11923
(914) 555–8877

July 26, 19--

Ms. Devon R. Nicholson
Nicholson Associates
440 Madison Avenue
New York, NY 12211

Dear Ms. Nicholson:

I constantly scan the newspapers and trade periodicals to forecast upcoming trends.

I hit a home run with a recent forecast, which will tell you a lot about me. I reasoned that, with the war in the Gulf raging, Americans would be traveling less abroad and taking more 2–3 day weekends. I reasoned further that they would more likely need duffel bags than leather luggage. I built our duffel bag volume from $25,000 to over $275,000 at this writing, and rising:

- I wrote a letter to 12 department store chains alerting them to the new trends toward "Weekend Gear."
- I placed orders overseas as well as with domestic vendors.
- I suggested the color palette, helped to develop 3-piece tote bag <u>sets</u> – and moved up our price point for greater profits.

I mention this to demonstrate I not only conceive profit-producing ideas, I also *implement* them.

As an executive recruiter, perhaps you know of a manufacturer who would like a visionary, money-making marketing specialist like me on their staff. I'll call you to arrange a time for us to meet personally, or I may be reached at (914) 555–8877. Thank you.

Sincerely,

Note: Once more we see a work-related achievement used in a cover letter to demonstrate above-average competence. The writer got the desired job with a manufacturer and told me it was just what she wanted.

Marketing/Professional Services

Brian H. Talliford
1321 Pine Street / 11K
Philadelphia, PA 31204
(215) 555–0315

October 24, 19--

Kenneth E. McCoster, Esq.
Managing Partner
Wickerham, Sharp, Sloan & Cabot
265 Park Avenue
New York, NY 12217

Dear Mr. McCoster:

Law firms often feel they are hampered by professional ethics from marketing their services as assertively as other professionals do.

How do I know? I am currently enrolled in the first course covering law firm marketing. It is being given at the New York University Management Institute by the Director of Marketing of Dewey, Briggs & Croft. My own background of success in this field, combined with NALFMA-sponsored events, give me a firm idea of how to approach marketing for a law firm, to wit:

You can expect to enhance your prestige throughout the profession . . . let present clients know your real worth . . . draw new clients to you . . . *cross sell your services, and introduce new specialties*. These are some of the results a successful marketing campaign will bring you.

For the past ten years, I have been researching, creating, and developing practical plans for professionals to market their services and build their profits and their prestige – in the intensely competitive environment of engineering and architecture. My present firm has doubled in size from 1981–91.

Because you are reading this far, you are probably interested in how your own firm can benefit from this emerging trend. I will call you next week to arrange an agreeable time for us to meet. Or, I may be reached at (215) 555–0315. Thank you.

Sincerely,

Note: A stong promise of rewards desirable to a law firm is made in the third paragraph. The promise is backed up by a record of success in the fourth. The writer told me he got the job he wanted.

Grace R. Greenspan
41 Westminster Court
Yonkers, NY 20469
(914) 555–1059

August 7, 19--

Ms. Ruth M. McDonald, R.N.
Chief, Nursing Service
Veterans Administration Medical Center
120 W. 23rd Street
New York, NY 11321

Dear Nurse McDonald:

Kindly accept this letter as an expression of my interest in the vacancy you announced July 31 for a "Patient Care Coordinator on 1E Spinal Cord Injury" unit. I presently assist the PCC.

I have trained myself in how to melt away anger. This is a skill very useful in the Spinal Cord Injury (SCI) unit. I have cared for AIDS patients who were not as angry as patients in SCI. I have cared for the geriatric and for the prematurely geriatric at age 35 or 40, and they are not as angry as I find patients in SCI. Dispelling their anger, I feel, is part of the healing process I can help to bring about. I am a very patient, attentive listener and empathic toward their feelings. And if the supervisor is enthusiastic, the feeling is transmittable to the staff.

You will see in my resume I have been constantly at work educating myself further in the profession. The Patient Care Coordinator is a natural extension of my present work, and I feel I fully understand its duties and responsibilities and can carry them out in a totally professional manner. I also bring to the position tact and discreetness in staff discipline.

The best I can hope to do in this letter is to express my interest in the vacant position, and to show in my resume my comprehensive experience in patient care and staff motivation. Thank you.

Sincerely,

Note: Please notice how the writer has focused the letter around the *patient* rather than herself. But it is still basically problem and solution. Problems are never far off, and every employer looks for people who can solve them. Only someone at home in the SCI unit could write this letter – it shows a profound grasp of the position applied for.

Administrative Assistant

Sonia M. Love
44-23 Ridgeight Street 6B
Ridgewood, NY 11311
(914) 555–2193

June 4, 19--

Dear office manager:

Perhaps this may not have occurred to you in just this way, but I am sure there are times when you did not want mere assistance in doing something – you wanted to unload the task onto someone else's shoulders.

I'm someone you can hand things off to – do this, do that. For instance, when I worked for the Queens Technical College, New York State inspectors visited our school one day, but not to get educated. They gave us 72 hours to correct deficiencies or close the school. I was assigned to institute new procedures:

The state said we must have timed admissions tests. I bought egg timers, and also put up a wall clock for students to see they got the proper allotted time.

- set up (then maintained) weekly and monthly log, with eight columns of information, to record each student taking the test.
- enclosed ten different books of test questions in plastic sleeves so they could not be written on and thus reused.
- arranged for testing site away from the Admissions Department (another requirement).
- ordered preprinted answer forms from the state . . .

and . . . I think you get the point. Give me something to do, and it gets done. The school stayed open, and was more efficient because of the improvements. Are you carrying around burdens you could shift to the shoulders of someone like me, and sleep more comfortably at night? I may be reached at (914) 555–2193. Thank you.

Sincerely,

Note: The author relied on two time-tested devices: the work-related anecdote that shows you at your best / and the problem-and-solution approach, which also shows you at peak performance. She got a call from the FBI (where she is now working) saying "We love your letter, when can you come to see us?"

Roberta Klein
2010 Kissena Boulevard
Flushing, NY 11390
(718) 555–0926

December 20, 19--

Ms. Julie Ann Sommers
Human Resources Director
Arco Aluminum Products
College Point Blvd. & Smith St.
Corona, NY 11324

Dear Ms. Sommers:

Whether your present office need is for space planning, motivating staff, buying equipment, or arranging a luncheon for a special function, I am fully prepared to meet virtually any office challenge that can come up.

I have met and straightened out every problem you are likely to find in a very large corporate office. I have learned the ways to simplify most office tasks and to teach others. I presently supervise a staff of 14. I go over assignments with them personally and explain carefully what is wanted, so they can make the best use of their time.

I understand the role the office manager needs to play to increase productivity and light productive fires under the staff. For instance, I purchase over $250,000 of office supplies and services yearly. I costed out what the company paid for these same supplies and services before I took over. The sum was $291,300, and the office staff numbered 19.

If you wish your office to be a place where employees are contented, and things smoothly happen, you will surely wish to interview me. I may be reached at (718) 555–0926. Thank you.

Sincerely,

Note: The role of problem-solver and the ability to get the utmost in productivity from employees is a theme you will see recurring in these letters.

Linda M. McGuerry
20-81 Longwood Drive / 13F
Westport, CT 21236
(203) 555–0341

May 10, 19--

Dear office manager:

One of my bosses once said to me, after I had calmed an irate customer, "How did we ever get along before you got here?"

I really am not all that superb. And certainly not an office star. But office managers need people like me as a general needs soldiers. My strength lies in my doing an awful lot of the day-in day-out office duties well, e.g., typing, answering phones, reports, scheduling.

I know virtually all the office machines in a modern office, and am acquainted with all the reports, memos, letters, proposals, invoices, purchase orders that constitute the information flow in a busy office.

I handled a 25-line switchboard and am used to phones ringing . . . many conversations going on at once . . . throngs of people coming and going . . . shipments coming in and going out – the complete administrative machinery behind a fast-paced organization.

You will see in my resume the above mentioned duties are my career. I am a career office assistant. I studied it in college, and in business school, and I am now a proven performer.

I always say yes to any new assignment, or to the expansion of an existing assignment. All my references are excellent, and I may be reached at (203) 555-0341. Thank you.

Sincerely,

Note: Once again, commendation from a previous employer is used to good effect. The writer of this letter told me she got an inteview almost every time she mailed it with her resume.

Martina A. Navilet
41 N. Plainview Avenue
Plainfield, NJ 25101
(201) 555–0159

August 6, 19--

Mr. Frank S. Goldie
Vice President
Marathon Knitting Mills
Route 14
Aberdeen, NJ 21341

Dear Mr. Goldie:

When I came to my present concern, I found nothing but bills, dirt, waste, noise, and confusion in the office and warehouse.

Only the noise remains.

We now have a thoroughly modern and efficient office and warehouse. I have trained an office staff of five (only two when I arrived).

I determine the credit status of all accounts, and can withhold credit when I feel it is imprudent to grant it. (I am quite certain you know how sensitive the credit manager's job is in our industry these days.)

I also managed the warehouse for one year, where I supervised a staff of 15. I increased shipping from 65% complete orders to 92% complete. I changed the inventory and stock placement, making it easier for new hires to locate and know inventory.

Throughout the warehouse and office, I set up new logs and records, and simplified others. I wrote up directions and procedures for receiving merchandise, handling returns, and other critical functions. In a word, the whole place is now *systematized* – and I am seeking a new challenge.

If you have an office or warehouse you feel could be performing better, then let's talk. I may be reached at (201) 555–0159. Thank you.

Sincerely,

> **Note:** Notice the letter's opening and the effect of using short (one-syllable) words: "I found nothing but bills, dirt, waste, noise. . . ." It would not sound nearly so snappy if you said, "I found unpaid invoices, squalor, extravagance, and pandemonium. . . ."

Administrative Assistant

Barbara N. Petrie

4221 Beechwood Boulevard East
Pittsburgh, PA 15217
(412) 555–7100

August 9, 19--

To those concerned with an efficiently run office:

I want to help you to run your office in such a way as will make the whole company respect and admire its efficiency.

I will help you in every way possible. I work wherever you need me, and until the job is done. I learn quickly. I am accustomed to getting instructions, then going off and bringing you the result you are looking for.

- I have an A.S. degree in Business Administration from Johnstown Community College.
- Know bookkeeping and some accounting.
- Type 45 / know word processing / IBM, Leading Edge PC / WordPerfect / Lotus 1-2-3 / Word Star.
- High aptitude for math / excellent number skills.
- Intelligent phone personality, for taking information in, and for giving it out (customer service).

I received a Certificate of Academic Achievement for "scholastic excellence and extraordinary dedication to self-improvement," and made Dean's List in 1988. All my references are excellent. I am never late and rarely absent. I want to be successful, and help you to be successful. Thank you.

Sincerely,

Note: This letter sings out the writer's great willingness to work hard and "be successful." A strong work ethic never goes unnoticed by employers. One office manager complained to me she had interviewed 26 candidates for an office job, "and two-thirds of them were prima donnas."

Peter Goodstein
12 Woodland Circle / 1AJ
Trenton, NJ 21710
(201) 555–1116

October 24, 19--

Mr. Philip J. Todd
Senior Vice President Manufacturing
AMC Corp.
1412 Broadway
New York, NY 10112

Dear Mr. Todd:

At a press conference during the 1990-91 war in the Persian Gulf, General Schwartzkopf, America's battlefield commander, told assembled reporters he wished to single out for special commendation the *general in charge of logistics*.

"He kept a steady stream of food and supplies coming, with huge cargo planes landing or taking off every five minutes," the general told them.

It is not too much of an exaggeration to say that fairly describes the behind-the-scenes role I play in seeing that over $100 million in women's sportswear breezes through the many stages of production. I cut and produce up to 500,000 yards of fabric at a time.

At the snap of your fingers, I can tell you what your factories are producing, how much it will cost, and how much money you can expect to make. I calculate the best way to allocate orders so you will be left with saleable packages by size and color, with an absolute minimum of unsalable remnants. This is critical in speculative cutting.

Moreover, I can spot potential production problems before they can mushroom out of control and put a crimp in your deliveries. You will see in my resume that my experience encompasses the *retail* end as well as manufacturing.

I have encountered and created solutions for virtually any out-of-the-ordinary situation that could possibly occur in apparel manufacturing. Now, I am interested in securing a position with still larger responsibilities, still greater challenges, and I may be reached at (201) 555–1116. Thank you.

Sincerely,

Note: Here is an example of *analogy*—demonstrating or explaining something unfamiliar by comparing it with something the reader already knows. The news-item opening also lends a feeling of timeliness and importance to the letter.

Production Planner

Ashish J. Gupte
94-24 N. Meridian Avenue
Merrick, NY 11374
(516) 555–1683

February 14, 19--

Ms. Linda Castle
V.P. Operations
Omega Fashions, Ltd.
370 W. 35th St.
New York City 10001

Dear Ms. Castle:

It takes years to learn the ins and outs of offshore production planning when the production team has one leg in America and the other in the Caribbean or India.

Even then, not everyone becomes an expert. It requires tremendous attention to every little detail, and a hundred things can go wrong. With rapid fire shipments and payments . . . large inventories coming and going . . . with the most exacting standards and requirements . . . customs . . . tariffs . . . import quotas . . . foreign currency . . . letters of credit . . . freight forwarders . . . insurance – you've got to know from moment to moment what people are up to, and it takes superb managers to do it right.

But the rewards can be just simply tremendous. For one customer, we built our volume from 15,000 doz. to 50,000 doz. Under my management, less than 3% of our production is returned for correction vs. an industry average of 5%. Let me convince you.

I will call you next Tuesday morning to set up a convenient time for us to meet. Or, I may be reached at (516) 555–1683. Thank you.

Sincerely,

Note: Please note particularly the *second* paragraph. The writer has used devices mentioned in Chapter 7 to create an atmosphere of "rapid fire," and ends with a statement the reader must agree with. He could have said, "superb managers like me." But understatement sometimes is becoming. The writer got a new job (and a 50% pay hike) from interviews generated by this cover letter and his resume. One of his responses came from a recruiter named in *The Career Makers, America's Top 100 Executive Recruiters*.

Katrina L. Solomon
55 Brookhaven Drive
Bridgeport, CT 41423
(203) 555–8743

September 2, 19--

Mr. J. Gordon List
Executive Vice President
Cushman & Waterfield, Inc.
555 Fifth Avenue
New York, NY 10021

Dear Mr. List:

You don't need me to tell you about the gloomy state of affairs in commercial real estate leasing these days.

Yet, I have managed to close about a half-dozen deals in the past six months, with several more deals pending. Moreover, five of these clients are working with me on an exclusive basis.

I did it through relentless cold calling. I make about 50 cold calls on offices every day. To get around being brushed off by secretaries, I call the executive in charge at 7:30 A.M. or after 5 P.M., when the secretaries aren't around. You'd be surprised how accessible these executives can be when you learn the time-tested techniques for reaching them – *and then asking them the right questions.*

Possibly you have a position in your own organization for an energetic leasing agent like me who does a good thorough job of cold canvassing and closing – closing deals despite dreary conditions beyond my control.

I feel that, even in these times, there are many deals waiting to be made. With an organization like Cushman & Waterfield both of us could profit greatly. Just grant me the opportunity to convince you in an interview. I'll be calling you shortly. Thank you.

Sincerely,

Note: The more upbeat, positive and optimistic your letter sounds, the more likely you are to put a prospective employer in the mood to see you. One of the ways to do this is to show accomplishments made despite a wall of difficulty and opposition.

Real Estate Workout Specialist

Bryan J. Harrison
125 S. Main Street
Poughkeepsie, NY 12601
(516) 555–3198

August 12, 19--

Mr. Charles B. Goldensen
Executive Vice President
Chase Manhattan Bank
Chase Manhattan Plaza
New York, NY 10018

Dear Mr. Goldensen:

Nowadays, financial institutions want to get nonperforming real estate loans off the books, and reduce the portion of their assets in real estate.

Someone like me could make a lot of difference . . . someone who can manage the loan portfolio, and restructure the loans or renegotiate terms with borrowers, when that becomes necessary . . . in a phrase – *a workout specialist*:

PROFILE

- Enjoys doing real estate workouts.
- Good at negotiating with borrowers.
- Skilled at assessing quality of real estate, and the marketability of that real estate.
- Understands the accounting, financial and legal aspects of the transaction, and the legal docments that surround it.
- Evaluates profitability by computer.

You will see in my resume the loans I have worked on are legally and structurally complex transactions. I have analyzed a lot of different assets, e.g., real estate, insurance policies, compensation plans for health care and benefit plans. At C.N.A., I was responsible for 40 projects, of which 20 were in default.

Perhaps you have a position in your own organization for someone like me – the workout artist – who has good *analytical skills*, good *people skills*, and the skill to make money for the bank. I may be reached at (516) 555–3198. Thank you.

Sincerely,

Note: The writer starts by mentioning a big current problem causing bankers to lose sleep, then, in the second paragraph, offers them an escape . . . so they read on.

Jocelyn R. McDermott
27 Dresden Lane / 12R
Hoboken, NJ 12016
(201) 555–2659

February 11, 19--

Mr. Kenneth H. Levitt
Senior Vice President
The Limited
32 E. 53rd Street
New York, NY 10013

Dear Mr. Levitt:

Not many retailing executives know more about store operations than I do, and few know as much.

- Have 10 solid years in retail planning, analysis and control / sales and profitability forecasts / projected one famous retailer's weekly sales within 5 – 10% of actual all the time I was there (resume).
- Powerful analytical and conceptual abilities to probe for profit-aiding data from billions in sales and $500,000,000 inventories.
- Comfortable dealing with executives at highest levels / write and/or contribute to speeches given by senior management.

I have made many major presentations of my investigative findings to audiences of executives. I enjoy selling my ideas to others and convincing people to take action based on them.

I know the department and specialty store environment, and the operating philosophies of the major retailers: Macy's (merchandise driven), May Company/Caldor (financially driven), the Limited (trend driven).

I maintain (as a hobby at home) comprehensive files on all major retailers, e.g., department store chains, discounters, specialty chains, etc., since 1985: know all changes in the stores, customer bases, sales, policies, etc. Which brings me to the point of my letter.

Perhaps you have a position in your own organization for a retail analytical expert like me. I will call you next week to arrange an agreeable time for us to meet. Or, I may be reached at (201) 555–2659.

Sincerely,

Note: This letter and resume brought numerous interviews and several job offers. Notice the next-to-last paragraph mentioning work done at home "as a hobby." Giving evidence of *devotion* to the work you are being hired to perform never fails to impress a prospective employer.

Department Store Manager

Lucas N. Oldenburg
21 W. 9th Street / 17P
New York, NY 12322
(212) 555–8914

October 16, 19--

Dear merchandising executive:

Praise is the cheapest form of incentive, but it is not the most effective. Money is.

I use both. I feel it is a major explanation of why departments / classifications I have managed almost consistently outperform the store as a whole (resume).

I trained and developed my five assistants to know their businesses inside and out – and get promoted. Before being promoted to my present position, I managed a staff of 15 for two years. Only two people left in that time vs. a 25% annual turnover rate for the store. I bring in bagels and coffee on weekends, and take them out for dinner after Christmas. I feel a highly motivated staff operating at their peak performance is where it all begins.

For instance, we built our flannel shirt business to 9% of sales in this classification (a $175,000 pick-up), even though ours was a 3% store. I analyzed past flannel shirt sales based on two months under my supervision and confidently projected a 10% increase to my boss. I added colors, styles and increased display space from 100 s.f. to 300.

Perhaps you have an underperforming store, product, department or other operation that you feel could be doing better. I am accustomed to working 60-hour weeks, and I love the business. I may be reached at (212) 555–8914. Thank you.

Sincerely,

Note: The appeal here, and it runs throughout the letter, is the writer's ability to get his staff involved. A motivated work force is an organization's greatest asset, and a topic made to order for cover letter writers.

Wilma S. Deluca
37 Windham Road
Forest Hills, NY 30011
(718) 555–0854

July 27, 19--

To the general/division merchandise manager:

Think of the profits that lie hidden in your womenswear area and what a buyer like me might do for you. You will read in my resume I took over two lackluster, underperforming departments and tripled their sales volume to over $9 million in two years.

I also developed an enormously successful contemporary area in a four-store chain, tripling sales in this area from $400,000 to $1.2 million in 20 months. With two assistants, I also handle all the administrative duties: maintain OTB / sell through / stock ledger reports / advertising / two seasonal catalogs / sales training and special events within the stores / and production of the company's annual fashion show.

800 pairs of fashionable eyes

If I very briefly describe our most recent annual fashion show, you will get an idea of the energy, concentrated attention and practical common sense I give to every aspect of my job. I flew to St. Thomas, and in four days:

- booked space in a private club (in exchange for the publicity).
- hired and rehearsed 12 models, with five changes each.
- picked all clothes, arranged for makeup and hairstyling for models.
- prepared and sent invitations to entire customer list.
- arranged for photographer, music, staged the choreography, lighting.
- wrote press release, prepared press kit, invited press.
- arranged for *hors d'oeuvres*.

Over 800 attended – seated in a space intended for 600, including several heads of industry, and the governor and his wife. There was elaborate press coverage. I made a video of the event, which was used for 1) company's TV and print ads, and 2) to be screened in the stores. And to link the fashion show to store sales directly, we invited attendees to bring their invitations to the stores for a 10% discount. The theme for this fashion show was the soft, graceful, feminine look of the fifties, but transformed into the distinctly more comfortable apparel of the nineties. I often get my styling inspiration by viewing movies of the period.

I am interested in assuming a similar buying position on a larger scale. Perhaps you have a position in your own organization for someone with my drive and practical experience. I may be reached at (718) 555–0854. Thank you.

Sincerely,

Note: The writer has used a subhead and a listing to break up a very long letter. Long letters will be read as thoroughly as short ones when they hold out as much promise of reward as this one does. The writer got interviews and a new job as fashion director with a well-known organization.

Ralph H. DeAngelo
227 N. Broadway - 17J
Fort Lee, NJ 21218
(203) 555–1916

August 31, 19--

Mr. Frank S. Pickering
General Merchandising Manager
Saks Fifth Avenue
570 Fifth Ave.
New York, NY 10018

Dear Mr. Pickering:

Several things you said in your large ad for an assistant buyer suggests you are searching for someone quite like myself.

I have worked only for better specialty stores, with upscale customers, whose taste levels are fully parallel to customers of Saks New York. I have the three natural ingredients required for success in the postion you advertise: flair, resourcefulness and sound business sense. Everything else can be learned.

I sometimes develop and implement two or more merchandising ideas at once:

Item: For Bonwit Teller, developed concept of "Prom Shops" – boutiques emphasizing prom gowns cheap and deep. Found a new resource to meet a $200 average price point, every mother's ideal. Worked very closely with D.M.M. *Made major presentations to 14 of the 16 Bonwit Teller branches, and they loved it.* Prom Shops would emphasize proms for two months, then evening wear in May and June, and so forth around the calendar. All the stores were very excited by the idea. *Asked for and got $800,000 budget to make it work.*

Item: Helped to develop three <u>exclusive</u> fashion items for Bonwit Teller's summer 1990 catalog. It is not so easy to get exclusives. Exclusives fatten margins and enhance your image as fashion leader. You can't claim to be fashion-first if you don't lead.

It's fun to see ideas pay off, to see the sales floor crowded with customers, to see the money collecting in the registers. If you like this kind of fun, too, then let's work together to build Saks's future (and mine). I may be reached at (203) 555–1916. Thank you.

Sincerely,

Note: The supreme optimism and keen business sense of the writer shines through every paragraph – and in his very upbeat close. Try to get these feelings of enthusiasm, optimism and ambition into your cover letter – because they are contagious, and may spread from the page to the reader. "They called me for an interview and showed me a stack of letters and resumes they had accumulated over a six-month period searching for the right person," the writer of this letter told me after taking the job.

Bernadette L. Russell
145 Leighton Street / 12B
Cambridge, MA 31497
(615) 555–9324

November 12, 19--

Dear merchandising manager:

Our 50 stores are enormously successful, while they are also very conservative about fashion and following new trends. And that is the point of my letter.

I feel I am more of a merchant than our company's tradition permits me to be. I would like to use my fashion sense – and merchandising input – to boost sales still more than I have done here. One example may serve as well as long explanations.

About three weeks ago, I saw novelty T-shirts that changed color from body heat. I urged placing an immediate order, and was permitted to place a $3,000 trial order. In checking with the store buyers to see how the shirts were moving, I got very positive feedback. One buyer told me the shirts were selling well even as she was speaking with me on the phone. The company authorized me to place a reorder for $175,000.

I also am experienced in handling all the administrative duties, e.g., stock reports / OTB / writing P.O.'s / quality checks / managing staff / and so forth.

Quite possibly you have a place in your own organization for a merchandising assistant with my fashion sense, business sense, and common sense. I may be reached at (615) 555–9324. Thank you.

Sincerely,

Note: This writer picked her biggest, most memorable accomplishment for her cover letter – a practice I heartily recommend. She got interviews and a new job that is a step up for her.

Director of Merchandising

Michael J. Levine
145 Union Turnpike
Pikesville, MD 01354
(415) 555–7563

August 19, 19--

Mr. Frank R. McCurdy, Jr.
Executive Vice President
Norwood Fashions, Inc.
240 Broadway
New York, NY 10012

Dear Mr. McCurdy:

You know how most people are – they stick to the beaten path. Once you understand their thinking, you can sell them anything.

They are willing to pay four times the worth of something just to have a designer's name on their behinds. You are going to read in my resume how I moved these same people onto a new path – "My Own" jeans – and sold millions of pairs. I came up with a sweater set idea and ordered 5,000 pieces (we sold 75,000 sets).

New products I developed constitute 40% of our $12 million-sales spring line, and 100% of our summer line. I developed a catalog from scratch and mailed 100,000. Company had expected the usual response of ½ of 1%, but is getting 2%.

I am seeking a position in merchandising at the division level where I can *really* blossom. I have a headful of ideas that can quickly be put to use to benefit your own organization. I plan to call you next week to arrange a convenient time for us to meet. Thank you.

Sincerely,

Note: This letter reflects perfectly the personality of the person who wrote it. It brought interviews and a job offer. Note liberal use of dollar signs, numbers, percentages, before-and-after comparisons to lend credibility.

Gerard M. Klein
415 Scottswood Terrace
Philadelphia, PA 18974
(215) 555–8437

July 24, 19--

Mr. William A. Rosen
Sales Manager
Bubba Creations
1401 Broadway
New York, NY 10011

Dear Mr. Rosen:

As a professional salesperson, I believe, as I am certain *you* do, that the true value of any salesperson is measured by the size of the person's order book.

But I hope you will agree with me, also, that growing the account after you've landed it counts for something too. You will read in my resume I made it my concern to know the GMM and/or DMM for every one of my major accounts. I identify and single out for special treatment *anybody* who can influence an account.

Our firm became the largest resource in our category for the May Co. And I grew our account with Nordstrom's from zero to a 30% share of their sleepwear volume.

I am seeking a sales position where my strong selling skills and ability to grow accounts in both good markets and bad will be valued. I will call you next week to arrange an agreeable time for us to meet. Or, I may be reached at (215) 555–8437. Thank you.

Sincerely,

Note: People are more likely to listen to you if you first agree with *them*. Agree with some indisputable fact related to the reader's work. *Show you think as the reader thinks.* Employers tend to hire people who are an image of themselves.

Sales Manager

Jason L. Love
424 Foxcroft Road
Kings Point, NY 11655
(516) 555–7766

March 2, 19--

Mr. Robert M. Fingerhut
President
Playtogs Childrenswear, Inc.
441 Broadway
New York, NY 10017

Dear Mr. Fingerhut:

I am writing to you at the suggestion of Max Hirsch, whom I met at your exhibit at the childrenswear show last month in Dallas.

This is about me, but will hold interest for you:

Item: For Childlife (children and juniors) – I built sales from zero to $5 million the first year, and to $8 million the next.

Item: For Doe-Spun – increased sales for one division from $300,000 to $5 million first year, and up 50% to $7.5 million the second (recruited for this job by an executive recruiter).

Item: For Russ Togs (children) – increased girls' division sales from $10 million to $19 million in two-year period / supervised sales staff of 20.

Item: For Tania Fashions – top performer among 25 salespersons / promoted to regional manager / then to national manager of children's division / division did $35 million of company's $60 million sales / supervised 20 road salespeople and five in showroom.

Incidentally, I have developed an index for predicting how much sales should come out of any town, city, state or region. I use it for forecasting sales projections for management, and for evaluating salespeople. Space won't permit me to describe it here, but I think it is something you might like to hear about. I will call you to see about a convenient time for us to meet. Or, I can be reached at (516) 555–7766. Thank you.

Sincerely,

Note: Notice this letter is filled with numbers, dollar signs, percentages and before-and-after comparisons – because business executives like seeing them.

Carolyn A. Greitzman
24 E. Clermon Avenue
Centralia, IL 30347
(305) 555–7843

February 18, 19--

Dear sales manager:

Here's what happens when I get a piece of information I believe has sales value.

A surgical nurse one day said to me, "Your company used to make a product to prevent cross contamination from one patient to the next." She was 65, ready to retire, and from the old school. I invited her to the hospital cafeteria to hear more.

The product had been in our line for 15–20 years. It was such a slow seller, we carried it in the back of our catalog. Previous year sales were $45,000.

I felt, if one hospital can use it, so can others. I built sales on that product – in my territory – to $1 million within two years. Hospitals began ordering 200 cases at a time. The product even went on backorder.

When management noticed the product was on backorder, they decided to run an incentive campaign to push the product nationally.

The best I can hope to do here in this letter is to give you a capsule view of myself on the job. I feel like saying – in fact, I do say – my selling skills will benefit your organization greatly, and I may be reached at (305) 555–7843. Thank you.

Sincerely,

Note: Once more our old friend the work-related anecdote is used to show a job applicant at his or her best. And once more it worked to bring interviews.

Sales/International

Martha A. Aldrich
71 Eagle's Lair Lane
Shaker Heights, OH 41231
(315) 555–9787

September 20, 19--

Mr. Hal W. Carlson
Director of Worldwide Marketing
Emerson Electric Manufacturing Co.
Sears Tower
Chicago, IL 32019

Dear Mr. Carlson:

I'm here to tell you it is not easy selling to the Japanese – for a woman, that is.

Japanese businessmen prefer to speak to a man. If you make a joint sales call with a man, they will converse with the man, as if you were not there. Nonetheless, Japanese businessmen became my major customers when I sold for TWA for three years in Tehran.

I took enough Japanese businessmen from Japan Air Lines to bring TWA's seat-load factor, Tehran-Japan, from 33% to over 50% (though JAL offered better on-board service).

Presently, I am No. 1 among a sales force that ranges from eight to 20. I make up to 60 cold calls an hour, all day if I do not have any appointments. I am the first in, last out, and I never take lunch. I love selling, and I never tire. That is why I am No. 1.

I close over half my sales on my first call. And my relationship with the customer <u>usually ends there</u>. I am seeking a position selling a product or service *where I can build enduring customer relationships and grow the account.*

Perhaps you have a position in your own organization for a peak performer like me – who can help you to build the business bigger and better through selling. I plan to call you shortly to arrange an interview. Or, I may be reached at (315) 555–9787. Thank you.

Sincerely,

Note: The writer uses two devices – the underline and italics – to stress her reason for wishing to change jobs. When devices such as the underline or italics are stingily limited to one or two to a page, as is done here, the reader is put on notice that the point being discussed is considered vital by the writer.

John L. Rubenstein
4225 Cold Harbor Road
Charlottesville, VA 51580
(316) 555–5167

October 29, 19--

Dear sales manager:

Are you getting all the new accounts you deserve? Would you like to take an enormous jump?

Several things you said in your ad for a hosiery salesperson suggest you are already, mentally, considering someone like me.

You will read in my resume six outstanding case studies of sales successes and bonuses and awards won. Here's a seventh.

My company was getting ulcers because for five years it could not get our line into Wal-mart with a police escort, while two of our competitors were on Wal-mart shelves, sharing the business and sitting pretty.

I stalked Wal-mart. I developed relationships with all four regional merchandise managers, who can make or break a vendor. I watched them more closely than their mothers ever did.

I got the Wal-mart account and started them with 28,000 dozen ($200,000). When last I looked, they were ordering 400,000 dozen ($3 million). I arranged with the mill to keep case stock on hand for faster deliveries to Wal-mart. I created a 10-pack promotion that sold 100,000 dozen.

When I started, our two competitors had 100% of the Wal-mart business. Now, they share 50%, and we have 50%.

I like going after new accounts. They make the job demanding, and you must have them to grow. Perhaps you're not getting all the new accounts you deserve? Perhaps your organization has underperforming accounts that could be doing better? Someone like me could be of real assistance. I'll call you next Wednesday to see when it will be convenient for us to meet, or I may be reached at (316) 555–5167. Thank you.

Sincerely,

> **Note:** This is an example of how a cover letter masks age totally. The writer is 63, but did you think about age until just now? The business world will drink up your youth and talent, and when you are 50, accuse you of slowing down. The writer told me this letter out-pulled his previous letter four to one in getting interviews.

Sales

William H. Schaffner
145 E. 67th Street / 15C
New York, NY 10102
(212) 555–4509

January 3, 19--

Ms. Joan A. Sonnebend
Director of Sales & Marketing
Group W Stations
2 Penn Plaza
New York, NY 10013

Dear Ms. Sonnebend:

Perhaps you have a position in your own organization for a young, ambitious marketing person like me:

- GOAL: Bring to a major stockbroker customers in need of financial planning.
- ACTION: Telemarketing . . . called prospects nine-to-five, and from 8 P.M. on nightly . . . called 200–300 prospects daily (set an office record). Rejection has as little effect on me as firing a pistol at the side of a cliff.
- OUTCOME: Got so many leads that the office manager asked me to stay on after college (I was a summer intern).

My present job for a major money center bank is to get very big companies, e.g., AT&T, to buy our bank's other financial products.

I single out AT&T because their pension fund is our department's biggest single account, and it is my account. Customer service – keeping the customer happy *after* the sale – is a kind of dogma with me. "We haven't been so happy as we are now and feel we are finally getting the attention we deserve," an AT&T executive recently wrote to my boss.

I am seeking a new sales position where I can (1) set new records, (2) have the potential to make more money, and (3) switch from the financial world to the business of entertainment, amusement and diversion. I love marketing/selling, I think it's fun; so why not market fun itself?

A year from now I will make you proud you interviewed me. I guarantee it! I will call you next week to arrange an agreeable time for us to meet. Or, I may be reached at (212) 555-4509. Thank you.

Sincerely,

> **Note:** The writer plunges the reader right into his major achievement then follows it with another. The phrase, "I guarantee it," is not an idle boast with two impressive accomplishments backing it up. The writer said, "The originality of my cover letter was mentioned several times in interviews."

Craig L. Ross
21 W. 67th Street / 12B
New York, NY 12117
(212) 555–1400

September 24, 19--

Mr. Sterling S. Bond
Senior Vice President
Smith, Barney & Co.
60 Broad Street
New York, NY 10018

Dear Mr. Bond:

There is only one reason for you to want to read this letter and my resume enclosed: It will open the doors for you to big money.

You will read in my resume how I opened the doors to Loews, Bankers Trust, Chemical Bank, New York Teachers Retirement Trust, and others for my employer. And that I was No. 3 salesperson nationally out of a sales force of 8,500.

Moreover, I have a way of holding on to customers after I've sold them because I steer them in the right direction and provide them with a wealth of guidelines and solutions to the fixed-income investment problems they encounter.

Perhaps you want some help in getting dramatically higher market penetration, or in introducing new financial products, or in merely increasing the business you do with existing customers.

The business climate today is not as bright and sunny as all of us would like it to be. But let me show you how to make hay even when the sun is not shining. I will call you next week to schedule a suitable time for us to meet. Or, I may be reached at (212) 555–1400. Thank you.

Sincerely,

Note: This bold, self-assured letter did indeed open many doors for its writer. It gets perfectly the personality, drive and *optimism* of the writer – especially in his upbeat close.

Purchasing Agent

Sylvia M. Manning
3419 Windermere Lake Road
Indianapolis, IN 51324
(617) 555–1920

December 4, 19--

Dear purchasing director:

Several of the personal characteristics mentionend in your ad for a Purchasing Agent lead me to feel you are searching for someone just like me.

I apply the same scrupulous attention to buying a $500,000 dishwasher as I do to buying a ream of paper (notice, *I did not say the same amount of time*).

I like to follow tested purchasing principles in my buying, and success usually follows. For instance, I rarely give more than 70% of our business to any one supplier. This way our company gains leverage and keeps them honest and competitive. Every salesperson always wants 100% of your account. Sometimes it makes sense to give it to them; most of the time not.

It is a kind of rule of thumb in purchasing to get the traditional three bids. I frequently go to six bids. On important purchases like the $500,000 dishwasher I like to talk to present users, see the product in operation, and so forth.

Sometimes you make purchases nobody asked you to. For example, I found we had 20 fax machines bought by my predecessor with <u>no</u> service contracts. I found that service calls were billed at $150 an hour. We were self-insuring ourselves, and because corporate employees can be brutal in mishandling office equipment, we were getting killed by repairs. I suggested to management they take out a master service contract, and they did.

I also screen purchasing requests to see if they are proportionate to the department's needs. For instance, with the fax machines, the more expensive models, with more features, are reserved for the larger departments where there are three or four times as many users as in the smaller departments. I do not place blanket orders.

I attend seminars on purchasing given by the Purchasing Management Association of New York that are profit-aiding in all kinds of ways. I will call you next week to arrange a convenient time for us to meet. Or, I may be reached at (617) 555–1920. Thank you.

Sincerely,

Note: This letter communicates the writer's enthusiasm for the work the employer wants done – a universally successful technique for gaining a prospective employer's interest.

Kermit H. Lambert
4561 Wisteria Court
Shirley, NY 11716
(516) 555–1695

September 21, 19--

Ms. Jane L. Ferris
Human Resources Director
D.L. Clark Manufacturing Co.
Robins Road
Union City, NJ 07861

Dear Ms. Ferris:

Several things you said in your ad for a Director of Plant Security make me feel you have someone in mind with my background.

Let's face it. The white- or blue-collar thief – the trusted inside employee – is more of a threat to your business than a burglar.

Burglary can be prevented, and usually is. When it isn't, the burglar commits the crime / it is detected / precautions are taken against future repetition. But the white-collar criminal carries a threat for the present *and* the future. Your assets dribble away week after week. All too often it can immobilize a whole company.

As a police officer, I have made a specialty of uncovering fraud, burglary and larceny, and detecting white-collar crime in corporate New York. I have specialized knowledge of its patterns. Most employees work honorably and devotedly and contribute to your success. But when one is acting dishonestly with you, it usually takes an expert to discover it.

I can provide detection and protection in all your important areas of activity. I plan to call you for a personal meeting to show you still more ways I can safeguard you, your employees, customers, and property. Thank you.

Sincerely,

Note: Here is a different kind of approach. Usually an employer sets the requirements for each position, for who knows better what is wanted? Here, the writer feels a superior knowledge to the employer of what is needed to protect the employer from hazards the employer may be totally unaware of.

Mental Health Counselor

Madeline S. Curtis, C.S.W.
24 East End Avenue / 16S
New York, NY 12128
(212) 555–1914

February 25, 19--

Ms. Harriet J. Ringgold
Social Services Director
Archdiocese of Brooklyn
125 President Street
Brooklyn, NY 30212

Dear Ms. Ringgold:

You may need a mental health counselor with my training, dedication and ability to follow through with even the most difficult clients.

I've just completed my masters in social work and my C.S.W., and have gained a variety of experience counseling alcoholic outpatients, emotionally disturbed adolescents and chronic psychiatric patients.

Let us look at other ways I can serve those who come to you for help. I have learned how to relate with many types of situations – hostile teenagers, schizophrenics and troubled substance abusers. Despite the problems on the surface, I was always able to engage them, <u>and successfully keep them in treatment</u>.

I look forward to working with your clients in the future and helping them achieve the most fulfilling lives possible. You'll find I'm thorough and effective in helping patients work through their problems. I would like to meet with you and discuss how I can contribute to your organization. I can be reached at (212) 555–1914.

Sincerely,

Note: The writer has underlined a single phrase. But it is an important one: One of the greatest frustrations to a mental health counselor is patients who drop out. Nobody gains.

Francine H. Sachs, C.S.W.
452 Lakeville Road
Princeton Junction, NJ 02145
(201) 555–1381

May 10, 19--

Mr. David M. Donegan
Social Services Administrator
St. Francis Hospital and Medical Center
Jersey City, NJ 20412

Dear Mr. Donegan:

I deal with despair, separation, anxiety, helplessness, hopelessness. And I believe I have the specific temperament, coping capacities, energy and optimism to deal with it. I like solving people's problems and improving their lives; it is a kind of passion with me.

My background covers personal counseling of individuals and families, as well as supervisory experience. I handle a heavy case load plus other duties. I am responsible for the entire social work section and its administrative duties. I lead staff meetings of nine or more professionals once a week to coordinate patient care among various disciplines, make assessments, schedule appointments, etc.

I wrote all necessary patient status forms. In fact, I wrote a manual, now in use in three other facilities, which explains – simply and clearly – how to fill out the 30 blank forms used by both the Jewish Board of Family and Children's Services, and the Special Services for Children division of H.R.A.

I also have excellent presentation skills. For instance, I planned a health fair exclusively for health professionals in the community and about 25 attended. I have presented before Community Board 7, and at a group of agencies that meet once a month at West Side Inter-Agency Council for the Aging.

I know my way around government agencies and bureaus. That is to say I understand their methods and their problems, and have the agreeable temperament to deal with them to get what our clients need. My background includes assessment, counseling, case management, and supervision.

I like the combination of both personal counseling <u>and</u> supervising – the clinical duties along with more administrative duties. Perhaps you have a position in your own organization for an assistant supervisor or coordinator with my abilities. I may be reached at (201) 555–1381. Thank you.

Sincerely,

Note: This is a long letter, but still it was read thoroughly and brought interviews and a new job. I hope you see the need to limit each paragraph to no more than six lines – two, three or four are better.

Art Teacher/Museum Aide

Claude A. Girard
14 Greenwich Street / 13K
New York, NY 10021
(212) 555–1213

October 11, 19--

Mr. Ralph F. Ingersoll
Associate Director
Brooklyn Museum of Art
Eastern Parkway
Brooklyn, NY 51678

Dear Mr. Ingersoll:

One of the most enjoyable diversions you can present to any child is an appreciation of art. It is grand and inspiring, and any teacher well grounded in it can teach it to virtually any child.

I taught art with great success to children in grades 1–6. My teaching consisted mainly of hands-on drawing, watercolor, collages and other art media. We regularly had artists in as lecturers, and eight times a year we had guest lecturers from art museums. Impressionist prints hung on the walls. In addition, I took the children on museum tours.

I *always* have had a deep belief in the interest and importance of art, a concern about it amounting to a kind of passion:

- Studied Art History, New York University.
- Ceramics course, The New School.
- Course at Met about the relationship between math and Indian design.
- Teach art to children, Oberlin College.
- Tanglewood Summer Institute – studies of collections for children.
- One-year course in Color and Design, Pratt Institute.
- Visited all the great art museums of the world.

I am interested in obtaining a position at your museum where my background in art history and appreciation will aid in increasing the number of museum visitors. Perhaps you have found as I have that there are very few people you cannot excite about art . . . *if there is enthusiasm in you*.

I am able to work a flexible schedule, and I will work wherever I am needed. I may be reached at (212) 555–1213. Thank you.

Sincerely,

> **Note:** This letter (which landed an interview and a job) once again demonstrates employers will make the time to read a long letter so long as it continues to be interesting to them. This writer sets out to answer the question, "Why would you be an effective teacher and a credit to the museum?" I do not seek to endorse long letters. The briefer the better. I merely do not wish you to develop a prejudice against them, judging *only* quantitatively.

Raymond P. Robertson
434 Twin Oaks Drive
Melville, NY 11746
(516) 555–9838

August 20, 19--

To those concerned with the repair of electromechanical devices:

Please take into consideration my application for employment as an electronics technician.

None of my competitors for this position can be more interested in the subject of electronics than I am. I have a background in basic electronics, and specific experience in electromechanical devices. Just give me a manual, and I can figure out how to repair and maintain <u>any</u> device.

I am also speedy. I was placed in charge of all repairs and maintenance for the Guaranty Trust Co. branches from Wall Street to 72nd Street – virtually the entire Manhattan principal commercial area.

I rarely was asked to re-repair any machine I worked on. I took completely apart office machines for cleaning and repairing. I set up and installed computers, repaired validators, adding machines and calculators, etc. I set up and maintained a filing system for maintenance on every machine. You will see in my resume I also have a great deal of experience in electronic security devices.

I am a fast learner – I won't be coming to you with a lot of questions. There is not a single electromechanical device invented that can scare me. Give me the opportunity to convince you by calling (516) 555–9838. Thank you.

Sincerely,

Note: Notice, the writer picks only two sentences from his entire letter to call to the reader's attention in boldface: 1) he is fast, and 2) he is thorough. Two very desirable traits in a mechanic.

Waiter

Billy M. Hannon
415 N. River Street
Cleveland, OH 30152
(312) 555–6413

May 16, 19--

Dear restaurant owner:

Sheraton asked dining room guests at its new City Center hotel (where I was waiting table) to write their feelings on "Comment" cards. I got the highest number of favorable comments among all nine waiters and waitresses.

I *read* the guests at my station to discover what mood they are in. Then I respond accordingly. I find it easy to engage customers in conversation on sports, wine, cerebral subjects, or whatever. I speak fluent French, and often French or Arab guests are seated at my table.

I am able to handle a large influx of guests with poise and calm; in fact, I am often asked by the manager to take over a table or two of other waiters who are overburdened. I have had the privilege of attending numerous management seminars on food, beverages, wine and service. I know, for instance, how to manage a guest who has had too much to drink.

Perhaps you have a position in your own restaurant for a real waiter like me, well trained in the highest standards of service, someone to whom your customers will be readily attracted and who will contribute to your restaurant's prestige. I may be reached at (312) 555–6413. Thank you.

Your success is my success,

Note: The writer promises the restaurant owner rewards for continuing to read: speedy . . . able to handle crowd with poise . . . will contribute to your restaurant's prestige . . . someone to whom customers are readily attracted. *This* is what is known as looking at things through the eyes of the employer.

Stanton M. Gold
91 Willowbrook Road / 5F
Boston, MA 24021
(315) 555–6882

June 12, 19--

Mr. James R. McDevitt
Regional Vice President
Oppenheimer & Co.
Boston, MA 25314

Dear Mr. McDevitt:

I have never been let go. Never been laid off. Never been unemployed. Never failed to make *beaucoup* money for my firm. And never failed to become a crucial part of it. You will see in my resume I was permitted to trade the firm's own capital.

I do all my own research. I am constantly reading. And I call management once a week and speak to the president or C.F.O. of stocks I trade. I also visit companies whose stocks I plan to trade. Last August, just before the big market sell-off, I could not handle all the calls from my customers wanting to buy stocks. There was no time even to make any cold sales calls. (I told my boss, "I think we're nearing a top.")

Anyone can make money as the market nears its top. That's no trick. The trick is to hold on to your customers and keep making money after the decline. The market has sold off 22%, yet I still have all but a handful of my core customers, and I am selling them new financial products as well as stocks.

For instance, at the advent of the Persian Gulf crisis, I looked at once for stocks that could be affected. One of several I found is Picture Tel (stages teleconferences on the ground for companies concerned with air safety). I went to see a demonstration of the company's product in use. Impressed, I called the company's finance department in Peabody, MA. I took a position @ 9½. (At this writing, it is 19.)

I am now looking for an opportunity to bring my selling skills to a much bigger organization than those I have been with. In a word, bigger *opportunity*. I may be reached at (315) 555–6882. Thank you.

Sincerely,

Note: This letter starts with the strongest message you can send to any employer, "I don't need you." The opening has six sentences, but an average sentence length of only six words. And, because 34 of the 47 words are of one syllable each – 72% – this opening is easy to read and brought excellent response. The device of repeating key words (*never*) in the first paragraph makes the opening still more readable.

Financial Analyst

Marcus N. Ogilvie
300 N. Winter Street
Albany, GA 30424
(404) 555–1900

January 25, 19--

Mr. Kurt M. Fleischer
Executive Vice President
Fidelity Funds Group, Inc.
23 Pine Hollow Drive
Atlanta, GA 30324

Dear Mr. Fleischer:

Several things your ad is looking for in applicants suggest you may be searching for someone with my background – keen faculties in financial analysis (resume), and *sharp selling skills*.

You've heard the expression insurance is *sold* not bought. Well, I feel the same about financial services. No matter how badly consumers need your services, they may be disinterested . . . fearful . . . or just warding off having to make a decision. Which is the whole point I wish to make in my letter.

Selling is as necessary to the success of a fund as is shrewd judgment in acquiring the underlying securities. I am a financial analyst who happens to also know how to sell financial services to consumers (18 lines of resume). Won't you agree with me that Dreyfuss and Fidelity are successful not only because they have performed well for their shareholders, but also because they are *constantly selling that performance*?

I have bettered previous results on every job I have held, and I feel confident I will bring you the results you are looking for. Thank you.

Sincerely,

Note: Another example of tight focus on a single subject. The promise of rewards is not always enough to move people to give their money to strangers. Many have to be convinced. Perhaps, some financial analysts answered by showing evidence of their financial acumen *only*. This writer zeroed in on the need for *selling abilities*, also. Try to think of how the crowd is likely to respond to an ad, then add an original twist of your own – which is twice as effective because it is *unexpected*.

Martin M. Peterfreund
4 Glen Oaks Road
Greenwich, CT 23050
(203) 555–1916

April 9, 19--

Mr. Mario Gabelli
President
Mario Gabelli & Co.
655 Third Avenue
New York, NY 10017

Dear Mr. Gabelli:

"... I don't care if many issues have gone up 30% or 40%. We aren't backing off ... says Gabelli, who manages more than $6 billion in five mutual funds and several partnerships ..."
  —*Business Week*, 3/25/91, p. 84

There's a lot of money in six billion dollars. You must have to put forth all your strength, and concentrate all your knowledge, to hold up a crushing weight like that. Can you continue to do this yourself? Probably. But there's no reason on earth why you would want to.

With every mark of the deepest respect for your stupendous accomplishment, someone like me might add many more millions to those you already possess.

You will see in my resume I understand the comprehensive role the money manager needs to play to uncover stored potential and maximize investment profits. I have provided down-to-earth, sensible, unclouded advice that have permitted clients to come out big winners. I unearth facts inaccessible except to the most determined analysts.

I can handle many of the functions you are often called upon to handle, without any real effort on your part. I will call you next week to arrange an agreeable time for us to meet. Or, I may be reached at (203) 555–1916. Thank you.

Sincerely,

P.S. My decision to write to you was not a random one. Like you, I consider myself a disciple of the late Benjamin Graham. His principles have guided me successfully through my career. Graham's valuation techniques were the subject of my honors thesis at the Wharton School of Business.

Note: The writer of this cover letter researched his celebrity prospective employer carefully in newspapers and magazines before sitting down to write. He told me he got a "warm response from Mr. Gabelli personally."

Financial Consultant

Patrick H. Abbott
234 S. Springer Street
Denver, CO 60828
(815) 555–5160

January 7, 19--

Mr. Harold F. Levin
Vice President
A.G. Edwards Co.
315 State Street
Denver, CO 60217

Dear Mr. Levin:

What do you do when overnight you find your own firm acquired by a larger broker, and twice the number of brokers are now going after the same accounts?

My firm was acquired by Shearson. Many choice Shearson accounts I had been going after were now lost to me. Do you fight, run, or shout for the police?

Here's what I did. I bought a lot of out-of-town directories, and started cold calling high-net-worth potential clients as far away as the West Coast. I set aside one or two days a week strictly for cold calling, and for visiting prospects (I drove up to 600 miles a day).

"I only do business locally" was a remark I heard seventeen hundred thousand times. This notwithstanding, I became No. 1 in the office at opening accounts on the first call. Moreover, I increased new accounts (over 300) for the office and for myself at a period when new accounts were dropping because of the merger. My manager supported me enthusiastically, and even agreed to pay half the cost of the directories.

I am seeking a position as a Financial Consultant where my drive and resourcefulness will be valued. I can quickly match financial products to a client's wealth and needs. I have tested phone selling approaches that have worked like magic for me and can be put to work immediately to boost productivity for you. I'll call you next week to inquire about a convenient time for us to talk. Or, you may reach me at (815) 555–5160. Thank you.

Sincerely,

Note: Once again a problem is presented as well as a strategy for its solution. According to the writer of this letter, "I had many more interviews than I accepted from my cover letter and resume . . . six people in one month said 'creative' . . . 'distinctive' . . . 'incredible' . . . and one man paused with his mouth wide open."

Norbert L. McCullough
40 Washington Square Park
Youngstown, OH 11424
(508) 555–2234

April 25, 19--

Mr. Thomas W. Walsh
Vice President Personnel
Foote & Randall Printing Co.
43 Front Street
Cleveland, OH 11023

Dear Mr. Walsh:

Kindly consider me for a position in your printing production department.

I ought to say right here at the start that I *love* printing. I cannot write another "My Fair Lady" or create a space shuttle, but I have very intelligent hands for stripping negatives and producing printing plates.

The printing trade suits me admirably. Every printing job, when you think about it, is a custom piece of work, and judgment is involved. I like coming in each morning so much I have 1) never failed to be on time; 2) have taken only two weeks vacation in five years. I am always where I am needed.

I am also a rapid learner. My company bought an Eskofot 7007 camera. The manufacturer's own technician came in to train me, and I was expected to train others. After a day's instruction, and by reading the 1″ thick manual at home that same night, I was producing with the camera the next day. With the NUARC computerized process developer, the technician trained me in the morning, and I was developing negatives in the afternoon.

Perhaps you have a suitable position in your own production department for a printer with my love of the craft. What I am seeking is a step up *technologically*, with a modern, automated printing plant.

All I can hope to do here is give you a summary of my accomplishments and request an interview. You will be interviewing someone who loves the printing craft so much I would do it free if there were not the matter of bills to pay. Thank you.

Sincerely,

Note: Devoted employees are something every employer wants. This writer concentrated his letter on that point with excellent results.

EPILOGUE

Even in the Great Depression, with its 30% unemployment rate, seven out of ten Americans were working, making money and buying things.

You can have a job if you want one. All that is required of you is belief—belief enough to take a chance. Enough belief to put the bold principles in this book into action. If you do just that—nothing more—the results will be hard to believe. I know you're skeptical, but I'm really confident you can learn to do it.

These are not theories on how to write a good cover letter. These are use-tested principles that have worked hundreds of times. The true value of this book to you, after all, lies in the response you get for your efforts.

You will now be able to write effective cover letters with no great effort on your part. You will be able to convey your ideas in such a way they will be instantly clear to anyone who reads them. You can enhance your image; make a lasting, positive impression on the reader; and get the interviews you want.

I know what it's like to be looking for work. And I know what it's like to be on the unemployment line. What I seek to do in this book is to make the job hunt more bearable by making the outcome more predictable.

—Stan Wynett

INDEX